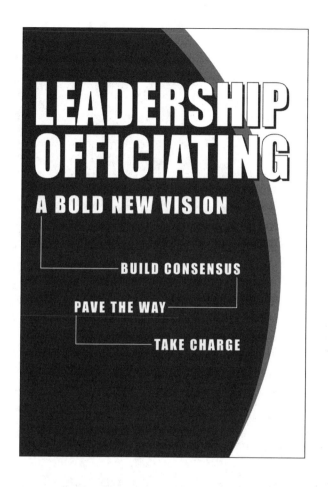

LEADERSHIP OFFICIATING

A BOLD NEW VISION

- BUILD CONSENSUS
- PAVE THE WAY
- TAKE CHARGE

Edited by Jim Arehart, *Referee* senior managing editor

From *Referee* Magazine and the National Association of Sports Officials

Leadership Officiating
Edited by Jim Arehart, *Referee* senior managing editor
Cover and layout by Ross Bray, *Referee* graphic designer

Copyright © 2006 by *Referee* Enterprises, Inc,
P.O. Box 161, Franksville, Wis. 53126.

Printed in the United States of America

ISBN 1-58208-065-8

Table of Contents

The NASO Sports Officiating 2005 Summit, with the theme of "*Leadership Officiating*," served as the basis for this book, supplemented by material published in *Referee* magazine and a variety of NASO publications, as well as information gathered from previous NASO Summits.

INTRODUCTION

A Bold New Vision

It's true what they say: "Good leaders are made, not born."

They develop through a never-ending process of self-study, education, training and experience.

Leadership is a process by which a person influences others to accomplish an objective and directs the organization in a way that makes it more cohesive and coherent. Leaders carry out that process by applying their leadership attributes — beliefs, values, ethics, character, knowledge and skills.

Nowhere in the officiating community were those processes and attributes more evident than in Salt Lake City July 30-Aug. 1 during NASO's 2005 Sports Officiating Summit, "Leadership Officiating," where officiating leaders from all levels and a wide variety of sports gathered together to share their leadership vision and learn from others.

Leadership Officiating was NASO's 23rd national Summit. Since 2000, NASO's annual gathering has focused on an area of concern directly affecting the world of officiating. Previous topics have been the official's role in improving sportsmanship, recruiting and retention of officials, evaluating officiating performance, methods of training and accountability of officials.

The program featured several perspectives on officiating leadership, including how to get officials to buy into a unified vision, identifying who is charge when it comes to officiating issues, what lead officials do better than the rest, the expanding responsibilities of officials and the eight critical challenges we must overcome now. Hot officiating topics were also a big part of the program as topics such as the use of instant replay, the legal liability of officials and conflict resolution were all scrutinized and discussed.

Among the featured speakers was NBA referee Bob Delaney, who kicked off the educational program with an inspiring presentation on the variety of ways we become leaders not only in officiating, but in everyday life. Dr. George Thompson provided an impactful session on his nationally-renowned conflict resolution program called Verbal Judo.

Other speakers and panelists for the three-day event included

Major League Baseball Director of Umpire Administration Tom Lepperd, Big 12 football official and Southland Conference Baseball Umpire Supervisor Jon Bible, Professional Association of Volleyball Officials (PAVO) President Joan Powell and PAVO Executive Director Marcia Alterman, Coordinator of Men's Basketball Officials for five Division I conferences Dale Kelley, Texas Association of Sports Officials Executive Director Steven Ellinger, NCAA National Coordinator of Baseball Umpires Dave Yeast, NCAA Division I women's basketball referee Anita Ortega, Big 10 Football Officials Supervisor Dave Parry, sports officiating legal expert Alan Goldberger, U.S. Soccer Director of Advanced and International Referee Development Esse Baharmast and Big 12 Football Officials Supervisor Tim Millis.

The NFHS family was particularly well-represented at the event with seven state executive directors either attending or speaking at the Summit: Ronnie Carter from Tennessee, Ralph Swearngin from Georgia, Marty Hickman from Illinois, Ron Laird from Wyoming, Jerry Hughes from Nevada, Evan Excell from Utah and Doug Chickering from Wisconsin.

Additionally, Larry Boucher, Kentucky High School Athletics Association assistant commissioner; and Jerry Bovee, Utah High School Activities Association assistant director, served as speakers. The NFHS itself was represented by Executive Director Bob Kanaby and Assistant Executive Director Mary Struckhoff.

The professional leagues were also highly visible. Current NBA referees Delaney, Violet Palmer and Joey Crawford all had speaking roles. Current and former NFL officials were everywhere: Bill Carollo, Doug Toole, Red Cashion, Jerry Markbreit, Parry and Millis all were in attendance. Current NFL Director of Officiating Mike Pereira and former NFL Senior Director of Officiating Jerry Seeman were both presenters.

All those leaders and many more from a variety of local associations, leagues and conferences put their heads together to discuss officiating leadership for both individual officials and for officiating organizations.

1

Are You Leadership Material?

In this chapter ...

- **What Lead Officials Do Better Than the Rest**
  The skills of the best officials can be learned.

- **How We Make Things Worse**
  Pitfalls to avoid on the road to leadership.

- **Leadership Comes With Respect**
  You can't take it; you must *earn* it.

"Are you leadership material?" That's the question that led off the 2005 NASO Summit. NBA referee Bob Delaney set the stage for the two-day educational program with his speech that answered that question. It covered the gamut from gameday leadership to the core foundations of leadership found in everyday life.

"Each and every one of us are leadership material," said Delaney. "We all have ability that we bring to the table, and we all have levels of experience. We have heard that when we officiate a ballgame, we should officiate to the level of our experience. I believe our leadership is the same way. Your leadership ability has different levels. My ability to be a leader is different at 53 years of age and the experiences I have than when I was 23. That's part of the process. What I say to younger officials is that you are a leader on the floor no different than a veteran official. It's just that there's a different level of experience in leadership."

Delaney's speech broke down the fundamentals of leadership into the following five core elements:

1. **Commitment.** "The ability to bring your leadership qualities to that crew is going to make all of us better. Individual commitment to the group effort, that's what makes a team work. 'Individual commitment to the group effort.' Vince Lombardi spoke those words many years ago to his Green Bay Packers, but they ring true in every aspect of your life. Your individual commitment, how committed you are — your commitment to being a leader, your commitment to being the best that you can be. Your commitment is going to show your fellow officials leadership by example."

2. **Communication.** "Listening is a communication skill. It's not only the ability to verbalize. Whether you're a leader in a family, in a corporation or in a crew of officials, taking in what someone else is saying is your greatest tool. Love everybody's idea for 15 minutes. When someone comes up with an idea at a meeting, when someone comes up with a suggestion, embrace it, love it, because we've all been at meetings where before you even get it out of your mouth someone at the end of the table is saying, 'We tried that 10 years ago; it'll never work.' That is the quickest way to stifle creativity within an organization. Allow creativity to come by listening."

3. Civility. "Leaders are civil. Leaders have manners. You know what leaders are? It's the thing that you were taught by your grandma and your grandpa, by your mom and dad, by your aunts and uncles. It's being polite. It's listening to a crewmember's suggestions. It's asking if it's OK to have the 11:00 meeting rather than demanding that the 11:00 meeting take place. It informs your ability to communicate, your ability to interact with people."

4. Ego. "Don't allow ego to get in the way of good leadership, but don't let it go away either. People talk about checking your ego at the door. I don't like that statement. I fly a lot. When I get on the plane, I don't want the pilot checking his ego at the door. I want that ego in the cockpit, and I want him being as confident and as cocky as he needs to be so that he can get his job done. What we cannot allow is arrogance. There's a fine line. Arrogant leaders are not successful."

5. Attitude. "Leaders face challenges with dignity. Every one of us has a challenge in life. I was told many years ago that we all get crosses, and that each and every one of us gets one, two, three crosses during the course of our life. Some get it early in life, some get it in the middle, some get it toward the end, but we're going to get them. You are judged by the dignity with which you carry that cross. Whether it be raising a 16-year-old, facing a stack of papers on a Monday morning or getting through a tough game, it's the attitude that we bring to the challenge that's going to help us get through it and show what type of person we are."

Those core leadership principles set the stage for the ensuing discussions. The focus of this chapter is on individual leadership — what working referees and umpires can do to improve their leadership qualities as well as the pitfalls to avoid.

What Lead Officials Do Better Than the Rest

"Let's not kid one another," said NBA referee Joe Crawford. "All of us know who are leaders and who aren't."

Crawford was speaking at a session in which panelists were trying to boil down what makes a lead official a *lead official*. In all walks of life, leaders just stand out. They have an aura about them that tells you they have things under control. People believe in them and are drawn to them.

It's no different in officiating. At every level, from Pop Warner to the pros, a select group of individuals projects a certain type of confidence. Players and coaches trust them, their crewmates respect them. Depending on the sport, they may be the crew chief, the referee or the guy in the white hat — but not necessarily. They are *lead* officials, and they are special.

There is no particular personality trait that makes an official a lead. Some command respect with an outgoing demeanor and a self-assuredness that might border on cockiness. Others accomplish the same thing with a quiet demeanor and a "We're all in this together" approach.

But all of us know or have worked with officials who come off as abrasive rather than self-confident or wallflower types who wilt under the pressure of a tough game or a hostile crowd. As Crawford illustrated: "Say I'm the crew chief on a game and say I have a rules problem. I look to referee C and he blubbers. I look to referee B and it's like, 'Bang, bang, bang, we have this, this and this and here's the rule.' I know which official I'd follow."

So what makes lead officials a different breed?

NFL referee Bill Carollo says it's an innate reflection of who you are. "You have to be yourself and it's about character," said Carollo. "It's honesty and integrity and ultimately taking responsibility."

According to NCAA National Coordinator of Baseball Umpires Dave Yeast, certain intangibles make a lead official. "To me it's confidence," he says. "It's a matter of the way they project themselves. They project to their partners. They project to players and coaches and fans. Can it be taught? I don't know, but it *can* be learned. No one taught me, but I learned from watching the officials who were around me and people on television. I learned it, but I wish someone could tell me it can be taught."

Today Ed Hochuli is one of the best-known referees in the NFL. His face and voice are seen and heard by millions of fans each week. But when he was working high school and college football, Hochuli wasn't thinking about being a crew chief.

"I was never a referee until I got to the NFL," he says, adding with a smile, "They got me mixed up with somebody else and gave me a white hat."

When Hochuli was starting his career he worked with Larry Farina Sr., who had a distinguished career in the Division I-AA Big Sky Conference.

"When he walked on the field, you knew immediately that everything was going to be all right," Hochuli says. "You knew that this guy was fair, that he knew what he was doing and that he was in control. The players knew that, the coaches knew that, his fellow officials knew that. I always wanted to have that feeling, that presence."

That desire is not uncommon in officiating. Who doesn't want to be known as a lead? NBA referee Violet Palmer says getting there involves a constant readiness. "You can work a thousand games where nothing happens," she says. "Then you work one big game, maybe something on national television, and you're needed to step up to the plate and, guess what? You're not prepared. And then you spend a lot of time in your career wondering, 'Why am I not thought of as a leader? Why am I still a U2?' that's the reason why — because you stepped up to the plate and you didn't even have a bat in your hands."

Knowledge and Insight

Projecting a confidant image and having the courage to step up when needed are great, but without a sound knowledge base to back it up, it's useless. In practical terms, that means officials who aspire to be a lead can't get there — absolutely cannot get there — without a complete working knowledge of the rules and mechanics of their sport. "Complete" working knowledge goes beyond knowing the rules, enforcements and mechanics; it means having a thorough understanding of how those rules, enforcement and mechanics play into the game, how they impact the ebb and flow and why they were written in the first place.

On more than one occasion during an NBA career that has

spanned nearly three decades, Crawford has worked with a partner who he says got "caught short" in a rules situation. "The people that know (that an official is hazy on the rules) are the people you work with," he says. "When the three of you are out there and there are 19,000 other people waiting for you to come up with an answer, you know who knows the rules and who doesn't just by looking at the person, just by how the person is talking to you."

"You can't fool your crew," Hochuli adds. "They know you better than anyone. If you aren't sure about a rule, they know it."

In terms of mechanics, lead officials tend to stand out, for good or for ill. It is not uncommon in some locales for veterans to continue to employ a mechanic that many would consider unconventional. But a lead official, while still standing out, will follow the dictates of the people in charge.

"There is a system that we work, and it's not my system," Crawford says. "It's my employer's system. I'm hurting (NBA official) Anthony Jordan and I'm hurting (NBA official) Michael Henderson and I'm hurting other guys if I don't work the system the way (NBA Director of Officiating) Ronnie Nunn wants the system worked."

Guts and Wisdom

In the heat of battle, it's easy for officials to focus on making calls and forget that they're part of a contest between highly competitive human beings. Lead officials are sensitive to the emotional tone of a contest and adjust their management style accordingly. Nobody is advocating letting the players run the game or not taking care of business. It's not hard to throw a flag or whistle a technical — it takes guts in certain situations, but it's not hard. On the other hand, it takes considerably more skill to talk a player through a situation than to take punitive action.

Lead officials, whatever level they're working, have that skill in abundance.

"You don't have to throw a flag to prove you're in charge," Hochuli says. "You *are* in charge. Part of that is keeping the players out of trouble. People are going to get emotional; people are going to yell and scream. If a player gets upset, unless they touch one of us, I'm going to walk away." It takes guts to walk away, and Hochuli is quick to point out that walking away just because you're intimidated or don't have the courage to take care of business is a completely different animal.

Look at it this way: The evolution of an official is cyclical. The raw referee may walk away because he or she is unsure, lacking confidence. Once some confidence is gained and the official's career progresses, the official may relish throwing flags, calling technical fouls or ejecting people. After that, a balance is struck between knowing which action is called for. It comes with experience and wisdom.

It is a hard balance to strike, but Brian Hall has done it more successfully than most soccer officials. He has been a referee for 30 years, held a FIFA badge for 13 and reached the pinnacle of his sport by representing the U.S. at the 2002 World Cup.

To succeed in the high-pressure realm of international soccer, Hall believes it's imperative for a referee to sense the emotional temperature of a match.

"The Germans have a word that means, 'the feel of the game, the feel of the moment, the feel of the player,'" Hall says. "During games, the top referees listen to the players. What do the players want in this particular game? In one game, there might be a lot of physical play in the air. In another game, I'd probably be calling that, but in this game, the players are not complaining. The players are playing through it. So where you draw the line is maybe a different place that night. The players are telling you where to draw the line, but you have to be able to hear and understand what they're saying."

As in any other sport, a lot of what goes into handling a soccer match successfully isn't in the rulebook. "You need to find that happy balance between managing by the book," Hall says, "and using personality, common sense and that feel for the game, a feel for the situation."

Confidence and Trust

Sometimes, there is a tendency for highly successful officials to stand apart from the crowd. That can happen when those who have climbed the ladder become consumed with their own self-importance. But far more often, younger or less-experienced officials are somewhat awestruck when they find themselves working with one of the big names in their association or conference, or when they themselves move up to the next level and are trying to fit in with a veteran crew.

When he is working matches on American soil at the college level or in MLS, Hall may be the only member of his crew with a FIFA badge, but whatever level he's working, he wants his crewmates to feel comfortable and step on the field feeling they are his equals, whether they are a referee's assistant or the fourth official.

"You need to have your crewmates feel empowered," Hall says. "You've got to make them feel important. A lead official has to have the personal confidence and innate trust in his or her crewmates to say, 'My success is predicated on your success and your success is predicated on mine.'"

Lead officials, he says, are part of a refereeing team, but they are also the crucial part that ensures three disparate individuals become one collaborating unit.

For all his success on the court, Crawford maintains that he's no better than his partners. "There have been times on the court when the two people I'm working with have saved me," he says. "That's what it's all about. You must make the people who you're working with feel comfortable."

That's a crucial difference between being a true lead official and simply being the "big dog" during the game. Most officials can probably recall working with partners who treated them condescendingly, whether by "taking calls away from them" during the game or ignoring their input during pregame conferences or oncourt discussions.

"I personally believe that's because of insecurity," Crawford says. "I believe that (some veteran officials) are insecure in what they're doing and they don't want to tell their boss or won't admit that they didn't know a rule or that a less-experienced official helped them out."

Crawford will watch over his partners on the court, but points out that rushing into a situation, like a knight on a horse coming in to save the day, is often unnecessary and can undermine a younger partner's confidence.

Humility and Empathy

Mistakes happen, that's part of officiating. But how a crew handles them can determine in large part how the rest of the night, or the rest of the season is going to go, and how officials handle a mistake goes a long way toward getting through the storm and coming out the other side.

"I'll deal with (a mistake) straight on," Hochuli says. "I'll say, 'That one's over; we've got to get over it. We can't fix that; we have to get on with it.' We have a signal we use on the crew to tell each other to stay focused."

If one of his crewmates makes a mistake or is involved in a controversy, Hochuli will keep a close eye on him. "We'll communicate," he says. "Maybe during a timeout I'll go over and talk to him and help him keep his concentration. I know he's thinking about it."

Again, a true lead official not only has his own responsibilities squared away, he's looking out for the other officials working the game, making sure they stay focused and are performing to the best of their abilities. So what does a lead official do when he's the one who commits a blunder? Crawford doesn't shy away from pointing out his own shortcomings when he and his crew sit down in the locker room for their postgame meeting and video review.

"I like to go in and talk about what we did wrong," he says. "That way, we get better. But I take a shot at myself. That's what I try to do. I take a shot at myself, at my calls, and then we can start talking about the crew's calls. I just don't like to walk in and say, 'You kicked that out-of-bounds play.' That's not good."

Desire and Drive

Whether it's through direct action or by example, lead officials are the de facto leaders in any game. Being a lead isn't just about getting your own calls right; it means serving the game by helping your associates be the best they can be. It's about confidence, humility and personal responsibility. But it's also about desire.

"I think everybody wants the lead role," says Yeast. "Everybody wants to be the crew chief. Everybody wants the big game." Lead officials can't imagine anyone ever shying away from those desires. It's that craving for the toughest role in the toughest games that earns an official the respect of his or her peers, says Yeast. "When someone like that walks into the room for a crew meeting or a league meeting, it's like, 'Wow!' The room just changes. In my role as a supervisor, I can't give any one of my officials that level of respect. I can put them on the big games and they can be very successful, but I can't flip the switch for that kind of presence. They earn that themselves. It's a matter of how much do they want to step up and really grab hold of a leadership position?"

Like Yeast said earlier, it can learned. But can it be taught? What's the final key?

"You just make the people who you work with better," Crawford says. "That's your job. End of story."

How We Make Things Worse

Now that we've examined what it takes to be a leader, let's take a look at the other side of the coin. What qualities diminish our leadership opportunities?

During the Summit session, "How We Make Things Worse," attendees brainstormed the most prominent ways officials and officiating leaders hurt themselves and the industry of officiating. Prior to the session, NASO conducted a survey of its membership asking those same questions. The results from the gathered Summit attendees and the earlier survey were remarkably similar:

QUESTION: What is the number one thing officials do during a contest to create problems for themselves?
Summit Attendee Responses:
• Arrogant and confrontational attitude.
• Lack of courage or a failure to do what we've got to do during a game.

• Lack of professionalism — how we carry ourselves, arriving late, lack of hustle, etc.
• Poor communication skills.
• Unprofessional talk, whether it be directed at coaches, players, fellow officials or fraternizing improperly.
• Lack of common sense.
• Not knowing the rules and mechanics and trying to function without knowing the basis of the contest.

NASO Survey Results:

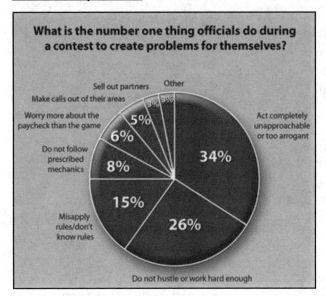

What is the number one thing officials do during a contest to create problems for themselves?

- Sell out partners
- Other
- Make calls out of their areas
- Worry more about the paycheck than the game — 5%
- Do not follow prescribed mechanics — 6%
- Act completely unapproachable or too arrogant — 34%
- Misapply rules/don't know rules — 8%
- 15%
- 26%
- Do not hustle or work hard enough

QUESTION: What is the number one thing officials do off the court or field to create problems for themselves?

Summit Attendee Responses:

• Criticize other officials or the assigners, criticize the assignments that they get.
• Lack of responsibility — not returning their paperwork, contracts and reports.
• Not taking advantage of educational opportunities.
• Lack of adequate preparation in rule knowledge, mechanics and

physical conditioning.

• Unprofessional conduct away from the game, such as gambling, alcohol before the game, smoking and chewing tobacco at the site.

• Double booking and cancelling assignments.

• Failure to adapt and failure to change — especially in regard to new mechanics or the move to using computers and the Internet for assignments and communication.

• Forgetting that integrity is a full-time job.

NASO Survey Results:

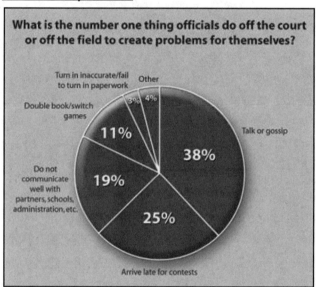

What is the number one thing officials do off the court or off the field to create problems for themselves?

Turn in inaccurate/fail to turn in paperwork — 3%
Other — 4%
Double book/switch games — 11%
Talk or gossip — 38%
Do not communicate well with partners, schools, administration, etc. — 19%
Arrive late for contests — 25%

QUESTION: What do assigners, commissioners and supervisors do to make things worse for their officials?

Summit Attendee Responses:

• Lack of honest evaluations or no feedback at all.

• Assigners not communicating with the officials.

• The "Good old boy network."

• Showing favoritism.

• Not communicating criteria for advancement.

• Lack of support if something goes wrong in a game.

NASO Survey Results:

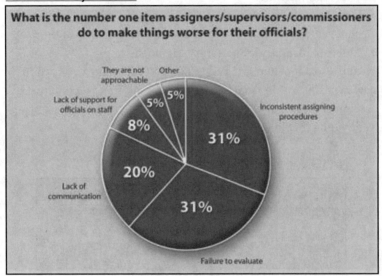

What is the number one item assigners/supervisors/commissioners do to make things worse for their officials?

They are not approachable — 5%
Other — 5%
Lack of support for officials on staff — 8%
Inconsistent assigning procedures — 31%
Lack of communication — 20%
Failure to evaluate — 31%

There is a competitive aspect to officiating that leads us to be our own worst enemies. Nobody does more disservice to officials than officials themselves. From badmouthing each other out of earshot, to cramming our successes down our colleagues' throats, to getting lazy and complacent with our work, to thinking that, "Yeah, I know what's best for this game and I don't care what my bosses or the rules say," as a group we're guilty of sabotage.

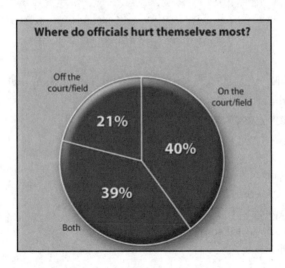

Where do officials hurt themselves most?

Off the court/field — 21%
On the court/field — 40%
Both — 39%

It's time to take a look at how our attitudes shape our profession and ultimately the games we officiate.

It's human nature, of course, and like most other people, officials tend to focus on ourselves, wonder how we can get an advantage and search for ways to get ahead. A little bit of that is nothing more than being human and, kept in check, it probably doesn't present any serious problems. Left unchecked and allowed to run amok and we have a population of officials whose focus is away from their games and on themselves and inevitably, the games and our avocation suffers.

It would be helpful to take a hard look at where we are and where we're going if we want the best for our game. Let's break down the most likely ways in which we, as a profession, can become self-defeating:

Getting a Little Too Friendly

The Scene — Official arrives at a game and immediately makes a beeline for a coach he knows. "Hey Bob! How're you doing, pal? How's the team this year? Say hi to your wife for me." Meanwhile that official's partner or partners stand uncomfortably to the side while the conversation deepens. Anybody at the venue, including the opposing team, can see the coach and the official whooping it up like a couple of old college roommates reunited.

Whether it's the officials who get too chatty before the game, the rec league umps who have beers with the players and coaches after the games or the refs who hang out with players and coaches in the offseason — you can easily lose track and be in danger of giving the perception of favoritism.

When officials develop an attitude that says, "Hey, I've been doing this so long — everyone knows me," you know they're in danger. Familiarity doesn't only breed contempt; it breeds familiarity, and officials who have worked games involving the same participants for a long time can let their guard down. It's as if they've begun to think the rules don't apply to them or they're needy enough that they're looking for friends all over the game.

Gossip, Sniping and Backstabbing

The Scene —A couple of officials are talking at an association meeting. "Did you hear about Chuck?" says one. "He's going to state."

"You've got to be kidding me," complains the other. "That guy is worthless."

"You're telling me? You should have seen him work the South game last week. Absolutely pathetic."

Meanwhile, Chuck ambles up to join the conversation. "Hi fellas. What's new?"

"We heard about your state assignment," comes the reply. "Congratulations, pal. You deserve it, buddy!"

You'll see infighting in lots of different ways. Guys will get the cold shoulder for no good reason. It might mean nitpicking on small things or it could mean petty arguments over something insignificant.

You can want the same successes a fellow official enjoys, but it's something else entirely — and much more malevolent — to want it and resent your colleague for having it. Sure, you can be disappointed, but when you turn that disappointment into hostility toward others you've crossed the line.

'Maybe I'm to Blame After All …'
What Do You Do to Sabotage Your Own Career?

A lot of officials are guilty to various degrees of making the larger mistakes of backbiting, politicking, playing fast and loose with the rules. Those are the types of things that make our whole avocation look bad. Here are a few that'll make any individual official look bad:

☐ **The poorly thought out letter** — Most states have a formal procedure to send in your comments about an unsportsmanlike act committed by a player or coach. While your responsibility in that area is not to be taken lightly, use it judiciously. Don't write up a player simply because he failed to throw you the ball after a violation was called. Be sure that when you send a letter there is sufficient justification. Let's face it, the more letters the state receives either from or about you, the more it will think that you are the problem, not a player or coach.

Letting Yourself Go

The Scene — Your crew chief arrives at the game site 20 minutes later than he's supposed to, rushes through a pregame (if he even has one at all), puts on his too-tight uniform, which was new when George Bush senior was president, and hits the field or court none-too-ready to work the game.

It's not uncommon for a veteran official to gradually drift away from certain aspects of professionalism. After all, as long as his onfield or oncourt work is exceptional, what's the problem? Plenty. When you start to think you know it all, that you'll always get games because you've been around for so long and the coaches all know you, you're headed for trouble. Those are the same types of officials who haven't read the rulebook in a decade, who don't attend association meetings and who coast along on their past success or reputation.

It is your job to treat your work with the appropriate respect. Think back to when you began as an official and remember how you used to do things. You got plenty of rest the night before, you got there early, you looked good and you riveted your attention to the action. You even kept yourself in shape knowing that would impact your performance. That's respect for the game.

☐ **A little knowledge can be dangerous** — Some officials are too quick to try to prove their legitimacy by enforcing "strange rules." Maybe it's some obscure bit they recently read in the rulebook or heard about at an association meeting. Their immaturity and lack of confidence make those officials look for any opportunity to make a ruling in an attempt to show their expertise and to exercise their power, making something out of nothing and wrecking an otherwise sound game.

☐ **Living in denial** — It's an embarrassing situation, but what is your first impulse after you realize you've made an obvious mistake during a game? Do you accept responsibility and move on or do you justify it in your own mind or quickly denial that it even happened? In football, for example, it's amazing how many inadvertent whistles "must have come from the stands somewhere." When it's clear to everyone on the field or court that you blew it, you do yourself the most harm by not owning up.

Singing Your Own Praises

The Scene — Local ref makes good and gets tabbed to work games in a big-time college conference. Everyone's happy for their colleague (or not; see the section on "Gossip, Sniping and Backstabbing"). What's the problem? Say the ref still works high school ball in another sport and he starts showing up to game sites and association meetings with his college conference logo prominently displayed on his shirt, his bag, his jacket, even the pen in his pocket. It's not overt, sure, but just to make sure you catch the message, he opens conversation by mentioning how tough things were in his last college game and how that nationally-known coach everyone loves is really a big jackass, and oh by the way, he might not be able to make the next association meeting because he's scheduled to work as a clinician at a camp for college hopefuls.

When an official shows up at an assignment and he's got the warmup suit, the briefcase and the collection of ballpoints from the last big-time contest he or she's done, what is the official really saying? The official is saying look how cool I am and how cool you aren't. Sure, there's some room for pride and there's room for passing on experience but you don't have to have the difference spelled out for you. You know when you're being big-timed and when you're the guy without a ton of big-time experience, it's a lonely feeling.

Playing With the Rules

The Scene — You're working with an official who says he's a "Let 'em play type of ref." Next thing you know, he's passing on calling fouls left and right, offering up a few warnings here and there — even on very obvious infractions that require no judgment. "Aaah! That's a stupid rule anyway," he explains.

As officials we have a certain amount of leeway in our interpretation of how our game's rules are to be enforced. A good official has enough in the wrist to be able to know when to come down hard and when to lay off a bit. The official, however, who gets lost in that grey area or begins to define all the rules as grey is doing the game a grave disservice.

Officials who spend too much time rewriting their own

rulebooks have lost their way and they put the integrity of the sport in danger. It's faulty interpretation and too much interpretation that hurts every official because it makes us look unprepared, incompetent and unprofessional. It sabotages everyone who has to make a difficult call and when the time comes to massage a rule a little bit for the sake of the game, it's going to make it that much harder for the poor official who has to do it right after the guy who does it way too much.

Sucking Up

The Scene — You're milling around chatting with some fellow officials before the start of an association meeting or a rule interpretation meeting when in walks the local assigner. It doesn't take more than a few seconds before you're left chatting with the wall because everyone's gladhanding the assigner.

Can networking be a bad thing? When it's used to enhance knowledge and experience, it betters the game and everyone involved. When it helps you form friendships and partnerships it's terrific, but when it's used only as a vehicle for personal advancement, it's nothing but shameless self-promotion and politicking.

You can tell the difference without much trouble. When you see someone who's friendly and conversational with everyone you can probably make the assumption that official is a gregarious person. If that official is the type who likes to socialize with others and organize everyone to go to dinner or a drink after the game, then that's fine too. But when that individual only hangs out with those who can advance his or her career and only makes conversation with the powers that be, then it's pretty clear that individual is trying to see just what he or she can get out of the situation.

Why should you care? Because it's another way the integrity of officiating gets threatened. The politickers are doing their best to move up in the ranks not by knowing the game, working hard or demonstrating commitment. They're doing it by kissing up and taking shortcuts. Thankfully, most people can spot disingenuiness fairly quickly so that technique doesn't always work, but occasionally, a very gifted individual with enough schmoozing skills can make his or her way to the top just by making friends. It's discouraging to those who just work hard and show up to do a good job.

So what is the answer? How do you get ahead as an official while still supporting the sports you serve? The answer lies within the problem itself — human nature. Good officials are made from people with good habits and good habits come from people who try to do good things. Take an inventory of your own behavior and your intentions and you'll have an answer to what you need. Just like every other human endeavor, officiating works best when the people involved are honest, fair and concerned about the welfare of others.

Leadership Comes With Respect

We've examined the ways officials can take the lead during their games and the behaviors that hold us back. It's clear that to be a true leader as an official, whether it's during your games, your association meetings or any other role in the officiating community, you must conduct yourself with the following actions:

Show It to Earn It — Professionalism and respect at all times are a must for officials. If an official is perceived as someone who slacks off, doesn't care about assignments or paperwork, whose comportment is below standards in dress, physical appearance or hustle, that official will not garner respect.

Support Each Other — As officials we've all been there before. The help we thought we were getting never arrived. Your partner has to be there for you. No excuses! While a partner or crewmate is taking care of business, the others should watch his or her flank. Then, if things get out of hand, they must be there for support. Don't get caught not paying attention or rolling your eyes when called on for help. Even a slight shrug of the shoulders is the type of negative body language that shows up your partner.

Keep Your Ego in Check — Being a flashy official is one thing, but drawing unwanted attention to yourself and trying to steal the stage from the athletes is simply arrogant and obnoxious. Other officials lose respect for officials who put their own self-interests ahead of the interests of the crew. Players can sense when you don't have the support of your partner or crew and they will notice if someone is out for himself. Far too often, personal gain, publicity and money get in the way. And then there's greed. Take the official, for instance, who will do almost anything to get ahead, get noticed and ultimately get to "the next level." That type of official seems to care more about personal interests and advancement than the intrinsic values of working a good game.

▶ **Stay Upbeat Off the Field** — The word "negative" has lots of connotations. When describing a sports official who is negative, the definition, "lacking positive qualities; disagreeable," seems to jump off the page. Those officials who constantly complain are really shortening their officiating careers. A positive attitude toward your league or conference goes a long way in opening the door to respect.

▶ **Own Up to It** — One of the most disrespectful and cowardly acts of anyone — and particularly sports officials — is lying. Officials lose respect when they show a lack of integrity. Don't try to cover up mistakes. Instead, simply own up them to the coaches, to your partners and to your supervisors.

▶ **Respect the Game** — Officials who show up to work games with a lackadaisical attitude or an attitude that the game is beneath them or that they want to get the game over with in a hurry are doing a disservice to everyone involved with the game and to the industry of officiating in general. If you're unhappy with an assignment, don't work it; don't accept it in the first place.

▶ **Make No Compromises** — If you have a foul, call the foul. Never forget that your calls don't determine the outcome of a game. The actions of the players determine the outcome of a game, so if the foul is there, get it. Don't officiate the scoreboard in a blowout just to get the game over with, and if you blow a call, don't ever feel that you owe something to that team.

It's not easy to put prejudices, selfishness, resentment, anger and fear aside, and nobody has ever mastered those emotions 100 percent of the time. Earning the respect and taking a leadership role doesn't come easily and it doesn't come quickly. You can't force it, demand it or take it — you must *earn* it. But the best officials in all sports and at all levels have their partners' respect and it shows in their performance on the field and their demeanor off it.

2

Institutional Leadership

In this chapter ...

- **Who's in Charge Here?**
  Identifying leadership needs and resources.

- **Help Officials Buy Into Your Vision**
  Communicating your message.

- **Building Leaders From Within**
  Characteristics of effective leadership and empowering potential leaders.

Leadership opportunities don't just come on the playing surface. There is a need for strong leadership in all areas of the officiating industry. Leagues, conferences, state associations, local officials groups, assigners, evaluators and trainers all can take leadership roles and all look for leadership within the community of officials.

Who's in Charge Here?

The question of who can or should take the lead on behalf of officials has never really been defined. Depending on the situation, the person or agency best suited to serve in a leadership role could be one or more of the following:

State associations — The state group seems like an obvious choice for high school officials to look toward for leadership. State associations license and certify most officials, and they provide regular testing. On the other hand, state associations generally don't assign or supervise officials until the state tournament, and many don't offer training, leaving that up to the local associations.

Leagues or conferences — Officiating supervisors or assigners or any other designee of the organization, including coaches, act as agents of a particular league or conference. Because they are the ones who hire officials for games and to whom officials directly report when there are problems at games, it's certainly reasonable to look to those individuals for officiating leadership. But such league or conference representatives are also beholden to their organization, sometimes to the detriment of the officials.

Local officials associations — Local groups provide leadership to officials in a variety of ways: Often a league or conference will contract with a local association for assigning and supervising services, which means individuals serving in those capacities come from the officiating ranks and are more beholden to the association than to the league or conference. Local associations also provide mentoring, training and general support to officials. On the other hand, local groups don't necessarily have the same amount of power and influence within a local athletic community as the state association, leagues and conferences might.

Individual referees and umpires — Officials can look to other officials for leadership. Even an official without any position power can serve in a leadership capacity by virtue of his or her status as an official, reputation and longevity. Individual officials develop relationships through the years, and can leverage those relationships on behalf of their fellow officials when needed.

Marcia Alterman, executive director of the Professional Association of Volleyball Officials (PAVO), led discussion at the 2005 NASO Summit on the topic of officiating leadership needs and leadership resources. Among those who participated in the discussion were Marty Hickman, Illinois High School Association executive director; Tim Millis, supervisor of football officials for the Big 12 Conference; Jerry Bovee, coordinator of officials for the Utah High School Activities Association; and Jim Jorgenson, director of the California Officials Association and owner of Jorgensen Sports Service, an assigning company.

The panel focused on the most pressing needs among officials and officiating leaders and discussed each in turn:

Officiating Needs From Leadership

• **Support and advocacy** — The group discussed who had the primary responsibility for supporting officials. "Most of the really good things that are happening are happening in local associations," said Hickman. "Our state association and other organizations certainly play a role in that, but where the rubber meets the road so to speak is at the association level. One of the things we can do (at the state level) to support associations is to help in training, to help in certification." To help that, Hickman said his state formed an Officials Advisory Committee made up of local officials from all over Illinois who come together to share concerns and help develop officiating programs.

"A second thing we've done in that regard is we have an annual officials' conference," said Hickman. "We learn more from each other at those kinds of events than we ever expected."

Bovee added that from the state association level, it is essential for the state staff to be accessible to the working officials. "We really feel that strong lives are motivated by dynamic people, and if we can assist our local associations in that process, through being there for training and leadership, those dynamic people will rise to the top," Bovee said. "We've got a group of Utah officials that are at this (NASO) conference. It's a heavy load for a high school official to be here, but they're the dynamic types of people that want to get better and go back to their local groups, and we need to be a part of that."

• **Peer leadership and mentoring** — The flow of leadership doesn't have to come from the top down, as the panel pointed out. Individual leadership and mentoring are forms of officiating leadership that have a horizontal flow.

"What we really need when we start out is the peer critique and the peer leadership," said Millis. "That comes from the people with whom you're working those junior high games or peewee games. You need to sit down and critique one another. The biggest failure we have is when we don't get involved in that, the peer critique, the peer leadership."

The flip side to that, said Millis, comes in the form of officials who don't realize they can be influencers on other officials. "If you're the guy who works the game, picks up your paycheck, picks up a beer and drives home, never says a word to anybody else," said Millis, "you're still an influencer. But remember that young guy who wanted to learn something, you've become a bad influence on that official. You're an influence for good or for bad. We all need to be peer leaders. We need to learn to talk to one another."

• **Recognition and feedback** — Organizations can offer leadership through simple recognition of officials' efforts. "Most every official I've known doesn't go out there for recognition, but I will tell you at least in Illinois we've done a horrific job of recognizing officials and we're trying to turn that around," said Hickman. "We do some things through our officials' conference to recognize people, and we think that's the least we can do."

Hickman added that the peer support from officials associations is crucial. "We think every young official needs a safety net, and that's why we think we lose young officials is because they don't have a safety net," he said. "They're going to have a bad experience, but associations can be there for the officials just to offer some support and feedback. That's what officials associations can do now to continue to leave a legacy and provide that safety net."

• **Tools and resources** — Beyond the intangibles listed, the panel discussed the need for a variety of real resources for officials that strong leadership can provide. Such resources include training materials, recruitment and retention tools and readily available information to make the officials' jobs easier.

"What about the need for legal advice?" asked Alterman. "That's certainly a need that we have both as individual officials and as associations. We all take this huge risk every time we even go out, and sometimes more than we're even aware."

Alterman listed several other resource areas that officials need to do their jobs properly: "Certainly we have the training needs in terms of rules and mechanics, but what about the needs that individual officials have in terms of, 'How do I file taxes? How do I keep records? What do I do for stress relief? What about my health and fitness issues?' There are a whole lot of things that are outside the realm of active officiating, and there's the need for us to lead in some of those areas."

• **Discipline and accountability** — The panel agreed that there is a leadership need in terms of discipline and accountability. Jorgensen stressed the need to have a formal set of guidelines when it comes to disciplining officials. "As the assigner, when an official does something that is deemed inappropriate or it hits the newspapers, the language is they are temporarily removed from the assignment pool," said Jorgensen. "We turn it over to the group leader in basketball if it's a basketball official, and the association does the investigation, the research, and comes up with the appropriate consequence. They report back to us, and then we take it from there in the assigning mode."

Millis added that discipline is a form of accountability and there are many ways officials are held accountable for their actions. Officiating leaders, he said, must have some training in those areas. "If you don't have the accountability, you'll never be accepted by the person you're working for, whether that's a seventh grade coach or an athletic director at a D-I school," he said. "And the steps toward such accountability have to come from the leaders of officials. You've got to have the accountability."

Resources to Fill Officiating Needs

After identifying the various areas of need, the panelists discussed a variety of resources from their own experiences available to fill those needs.

Providing the tools and the setting for leadership to emerge — "One of the things that we've been able to do is provide some grant money for associations to start mentoring programs and recruitment programs," said Hickman. "We've also reached out to universities and high schools to conduct officiating classes. We've tried to put some of our resources back into developing officiating programs. In some ways you can determine whether leadership is there or not if the actions really match your convictions. Well, we believe so strongly in the fact that officials are key to our interscholastic experience and it being a positive interscholastic experience, we're committed to making sure our actions and our convictions are one and the same."

Bovee stressed the importance of consistency in helping to guide local associations. "We've tried hard to develop some curriculum that's consistent each week in all of our associations statewide so that we're all on the same page, so that there's a unified effort in our education," he said.

Jorgensen echoed Bovee's message, relating his experience in California. "A great resource is the California Basketball Officials Association. They have a wonderful educational training manual that probably 95 percent of the associations in California follow. It is the prescribed training manual for basketball officials in the state of California. Nevada has joined and many of their associations belong to it, and it's available to other associations and groups to purchase to use for instructional material."

The group noted the presence of national organizations, such as the NFHS, NCAA, PAVO, USSF and others that provide another layer of leadership in officiating. "We have tremendous resources through the NFHS," said Carter. "If I think about just in the last decade the changes that have been made at the National Federation, and I think back to the transparencies we were using when I first came into the office, and now the things that we have with the PowerPoints and the interactive things that are going on. Those are huge resource for all of us who work with high school folks."

Combating abuses of power — Leadership can have its dark side if leaders aren't using their power effectively or if a system of leadership becomes a closed "old boy" network. "We've found that when the president is the assigner and the leader in an association, there can often be problems, because there's no balance of authority

Communicate Your Vision

Association leadership has an awesome responsibility to its members. It is easy for the leadership to get bogged down in the details. If you want a motivated group of ever-improving officials, you should have a vision of where you want the group to go. More important, you must communicate your vision to the membership.

A vision message must have five key elements:

1. **Authenticity**
2. **Relevance**
3. **Foresight**
4. **Focus**
5. **Interdependence.**

If your vision is for everyone to work to their full potential and improve their skills, you are being genuine. If you show them a training plan for the next 12 months and they can see how they will get valuable training on every aspect of the game, they will become believers. If you promise everyone a state final playoff assignment, they will quickly tune your message out.

Show relevance by bringing your plans to the right level. If your association or balance of power so to speak," said Bovee. "What we did to counteract that was we took our varsity assigner outside of the local association and hired that person as an agent. Our schools came to us and said we would like to have some crossover between the associations. So we hired an assigner who basically assigns across those several associations. The schools hire him and he's independent of the local associations. It's worked very well for us to try to balance out that power. Now, do all of our associations like that setup? No, they don't, because they're not in a position all the time to matriculate the people through the system that they see, so they have to work together. But it has worked good to balance that out and get more people involved in that process for us."

Millis warned of the dangers of not having the right person in a position of leadership. "The worst thing you can do is take on a role on

covers high school ball, talk of the NBA and NHL does little good. Aim training, ethics, mechanics and man-management at what your members find at the high school level.

Your vision must have foresight. Focus in the far distant future, much like a beacon on the horizon. Plan your strategy so members are not held back when they are ready to advance, so no members are rushed into contests that are over their heads. The consequences of rushing members: You often have one less member.

Focus your vision on a few key areas. "Guys, we may not be NBA refs, but no one can ever accuse any of us of not hustling or using poor, unauthorized mechanics." It may be that simple. Get every member of the organization to accept and adopt those two key areas. Make it a point of pride.

Interdependence among members helps them achieve the goals together. Let's suppose your vision includes never being out-hustled. A few members start hitting the track once a week to train; they see how much easier it is to stay with the athletes. A few coaches comment on their fitness. Those comments make their way back to the association leaders, who mention them at a regular meeting. Some more folks find the track and arrange to work out together. Your vision becomes reality.

Keep your vision authentic, relevant and focused. Use foresight and allow the members to depend on one another for success.

a committee or as an officer of a local association and not have the time or the interest to really do it. They're counting on you to do it; you need to do it. So if you don't have the time and don't have the interest based on your present situation, you need to stay away from those jobs. So often we get officers and leaders and assigners involved in associations because we've got the best political machine. This is somewhat of a paradox, because on those positions where you're elected, even the good officer, the good leader, has got to have somewhat of a politician to be elected. Where you run into real problems is a person who's not a very good president or assigner, but he's a damn good politician, and you can't beat him. That's where I think we have to really take a look at how we get things done to make sure we're providing the right leadership to the various groups of officials."

Where are new leaders coming from? — By recruiting new officials, Alterman noted, we also recruit new leaders. "A great referee is not necessarily a great leader in other roles," she said. "So we have to get people into the system to find out what their skill set is and what they can bring to our entire community, and then borrow from that skill set to plug them into the spot where they fit the best, whether it's the best person to be on the floor, or the best person to be running my association, or the best person to be developing a mentoring system. I have to be able to identify those skills and make sure that those skills are being used in the best way they can."

Help Officials Buy Into Your Vision

It's a question constant in the minds of association leaders throughout the country, "How can I get our officials to buy into my vision?" Not an easy task. However, there were many ideas presented at NASO's Summit to help provide a basis for local association leaders throughout the country. NASO brought together some of the leaders in their respective sports to discuss different alternatives and ideas on leadership and styles that will help you effectively communicate to your association.

The panel included Dave Yeast, NCAA national coordinator of baseball umpires; Larry Boucher, Kentucky High School Athletic

Association assistant commissioner and NFHS basketball rules chair; Marcy Weston, NCAA coordinator of women's basketball officials; Ben Jay, Pac-10 Conference assistant commissioner; and was moderated by Joan Powell, president of PAVO.

Each of the panelists weighed in on their beliefs as to what works for them as a leader. "More than anything else, the one thing that has helped me in my position is to be a consensus builder," said Yeast. "I work with my coordinators and officials to empower them and make them feel like they do have a voice in our program and our process."

Similar sentiments were echoed by Weston, who recently announced her retirement after 21 years of service in an NCAA leadership role. "I'm very big on feedback from the people I lead or direct. I read every comment on our surveys at the end of the year and use those comments to formulate my plans for the next year."

Being in a leadership position can be difficult, but it is important that the officials you are working with believe you have an interest in their well-being according to Boucher. "I think they have to believe that you want them to be the best they can be and that you have a vision about how to do that," h said. "I don't believe officials always need to like you, but they need to believe in you. And if they do, they will follow."

Moving into a leadership position within an organization does not automatically command that respect. Leaders need to earn that respect. Jay, an administrator within the Pac-10 office, gets the opportunity to deal with many different levels of leaders on a weekly basis. "By far, the leaders most difficult to work with are the those persons who have huge egos and think they're owed respect. I emphasize *owed*," said Jay.

Weston also offered one compelling similarity between poor leadership styles involved a lack of flexibility. "It's nice if you can demand everything and people do it exactly the way that you want it. But it's not reality and gets so many people in trouble within leadership positions." Some of that can be traced back to the previous point with leaders who let egos get in the way and have not earned a true amount of respect from their peers.

So much of what was discussed went back to earning a level of respect within that leadership position. According to Boucher, "The best supervisors or association leaders I've met understand the heart of an official. That's why, as a general rule, the best have an officiating background and experience. They understand what officials are going through and know how to respond accordingly."

A major consensus among the group revolved around the toughest aspect of an officiating leader's job. The overwhelming response dealt with the discipline needed to provide constructive and critical evaluations. It can be easy to let emotions and personal feelings in the way, but it remains crucial that evaluations within any organization are set up with discipline. Those evaluations should be accurate and should not be made based upon politics or bias.

Building Leaders From Within

Those who have had the call to be a leader within the officiating community know the time and effort involved with leadership positions. More importantly we need to realize the true nature of leadership. You can't be a leader if you can't encourage people to follow. There are some specific characteristics that will help ensure that an elected representative becomes a true leader.

Characteristics of Effective Leadership

Service attitude. Too many people believe that the call to leadership is about *power* and having the opportunity to interject our personal agenda and shape the group according to our plan or desire. But leadership isn't about power; it's about *service*. With a service attitude and demeanor, we are working toward the development and progress of each individual member. Typically, leaders are elected through some type of democratic process. In essence, we are elected to represent the group not ourselves. The association goes as the leadership directs. A service orientation is a solid basis for a successful association.

Vision. A leader needs to have a clear idea of where the group is headed. The direction needs to be formulated by the group after considering the specific needs of its members and the schools, conferences, leagues or state activities association that it serves.

A strong leader is persistent in articulating and following the vision. We will never get where we are headed if we don't know where we are going or don't work toward our goals.

Passion. True leaders are passionate about the success of the group. They are passionate about the goals and mission of the group. That passion must be communicated to members and other constituents. People need to see that we are excited, committed and driven to promote the appropriate success of the group.

Integrity. There is a strong need for a leader to be a person of integrity. No one wants to put his or her faith and trust in a person who is unreliable or untruthful. It is essential to do what you say that you are going to do. Don't make rash promises or sweeping statements. Say what you mean and mean what you say. A large part of integrity involves knowing yourself. As a leader, you don't need to be the best official; you need to be the one above reproach. People are very understanding and forgiving about shortcomings or faults; no one is understanding or forgiving of lies.

Communication. Real communication is rooted not in talking and writing, but in listening. An effective leadership group can talk freely about problems and issues without worrying about petty politics and tender egos. Remember, there is a difference between aggressive and disrespectful arguments and open and honest debate! The group must also have its finger on the pulse of the masses. What are the expectations of their customers (association members, coaches, school administrators)? Listen to their complaints with an open mind. Seek clarity. Repeat what you heard to confirm you heard it and understood what they wanted to say. Ask the probing question to understand the real problem. Ask their opinions on what they believe the right path to solving the problem will be. Encourage them to work with leadership to solve the problem or resolve the issue.

Candor. A leader needs to be very candid. An honesty of thought and action is essential. So is kindness. Kindness is an important element to keep in consideration when being candid. We need to be honest, but also kind. We can be direct and firm, but do not need to be brutal in honesty.

Trust. It's a product of integrity. Trust is a two-way street. We need to trust the people we serve, and they need to be able to trust us in return. An environment of trust is established by allowing decisions to be made at the lowest possible level. A true leader establishes and articulates guidelines and then promotes autonomy. Everyone can be involved in the process. A leader is not a dictator, but demonstrates a trust of the opinions and abilities of the group.

Genuine concern for others. Leaders have sincere care for the people they serve. We won't like everyone we encounter; it's part of life. As leaders, though, we need to respect and to be concerned about each member in the group. It is not our place to ridicule or demean. We must project a demeanor that is welcoming and sincere.

If we practice and strive to make those specific leadership qualities a part of our personality, we can become effective leaders and help the entire officiating industry strive to achieve common goals.

Empowering Your Potential Leaders

We generally think of officiating leadership as assigning power, elected power and the power to garner the best assignments (which presumably is linked to ability). That traditional power can translate

So Now You're in Charge
How to Make a Realistic Impact as a New Leader

Congratulations, president, you've won the election! If you are like most folks who run for the senior leadership position in an officials organization, you want to make some changes to the way things are done. You convinced enough people that you are the right person with the right message. You have fire in your belly, driven by a mandate to make swift changes to improve your group. You've thought long and hard about what needs to be changed and you are committed to making those things happen on your watch.

Consider the two lists to the right. Pick one thing to change and do it well. Put together a team of advisors including some who disagree with your position. Develop your purposeful direction in clear and concise terms and explain it to your team. Once everyone understands what you're trying to accomplish, refine it by listening carefully to all points of view ensuring you hear all sides. That will give you buy-in from the group.

Now that you have a broad base of support, you and your team must develop the action plan to get there. Delegate parts of the plan to your team and solicit other volunteers from your association. The hardest part of delegation is letting the people to whom you delegated do their jobs.

When you delegate the task, make sure the task is understood and the reporting requirements are clear to everyone. Be available for consultation when the team gets stuck. Learn to ask open-ended, thought-provoking questions to help the team get unstuck. Do not give them the answer. Let the team sort it out with your guidance. That way, the team has ownership of the problem and the solution.

To be a successful leader in a volunteer organization, remember everyone there is motivated to be there, has generally the same reason to attend as you do and wants to be treated as a professional.

into economic power — the power to run camps, give clinics etc. It can translate into power to be a trainer in your association — a power that gives one access to all the new officials, which should reinforce one's power to assign, be elected and garner future good assignments when the best of the new officials move into future leadership positions. Traditional power can translate into a lot. However, that traditional power isn't the only source of leadership within an officiating group.

Associations have many potential leaders. Those potential leaders are often just sitting there waiting for the association to empower them by asking them to exercise leadership.

Associations need to allow their members to use their professional skills on behalf of the association. Associations have members who are insurance agents, actuaries, police officers, firefighters, teachers, attorneys, marketing people, website designers, dentists and store owners, among others.

Those professionals should be used! An association should ask the

Keys to Success as a Leader
- Remember people follow those who communicate well and often.
- People follow those who listen to their points of view and consider their input.
- People want a sense of purposeful direction.
- People need to know the end result and how that will make their lives better.
- People need a plan of action that takes them from where they are to where they should be.
- People need to know you care and have their best interest at heart.
- When things go wrong, people need to know you are working to get things back on track.
- People demand accountability and acceptance of responsibility. Respect is earned.

Roadblocks to Success as a Leader
- You are elected for one perhaps two years. Reorganizing everything is too big.
- Change is easy to talk about and difficult to implement.
- Your other team members also have an agenda for change.
- Generally people in organizations accept the status quo.
- Officials are volunteers and can easily vote with their feet.
- Effective leadership takes time and patience to bring constituents to your side.
- There is always another potential leader waiting in the wings, hoping for you to fail.
- The membership isn't the only beast that needs to be fed. You may be beholden to other individuals and entities.

attorney, the actuary and the insurance agent to work on improving game contracts and association bylaws. The website designer can work on the group's website. The teachers may not be able to solve the problem at a school, but they can provide valuable insight. The marketing person may be able to help you recruit by getting you radio airtime or a piece in the newspaper. The police officers may be able to work with the tough schools to enhance game security and to ensure the security of the association members at games.

Almost all associations are willing to use those professionals once they rise to an acceptable level of association leadership. Associations are generally more than happy to ask the marketing person for help once she's become a playoff official even if she's not yet a state championship official. The challenge for associations is to find a way to use the second-year, non-playoff official who is also a marketing person. That person may have leadership skills to offer the association, too. That potential leader needs to be empowered for the good of the association.

An association faces some challenges in empowering leaders who do not hold traditional leadership roles in an association. After all, associations are comfortable with the people who hold traditional leadership positions. They know that the association assigner has been around 40 years and just isn't going to give himself the big games. They know that the president is respected in his real job. Those people are safe. Nothing crazy or awful is going to happen.

An association has to take a number of steps to protect itself before it tries to empower its non-traditional leaders. First, an association needs to do a little research to make sure that the people are good in their professions. After all, you wouldn't want an association to empower someone who isn't respected within their field. The disbarred attorney or suspended dentist is probably not the guy your group wants to empower. The local businessman who just embezzled company funds is not the guy you want to empower to help with contracts.

At the same time, an association needs to make sure that inexperienced officials don't expect some quid pro quo when an association empowers them to use their business skills to help the association. The radio DJ who got your association a radio spot that led to a 75 percent increase in recruits shouldn't expect the state finals when she's only a third-year official with no playoff experience.

To ensure there is no "I'll scratch your back, you scratch mine" dealing going on, it should do what associations should always be doing — have strong evaluation systems; provide the evaluations to the members; have an appeal process in case someone disagrees with an evaluation; link assigning to evaluations; have training that allows officials to get better; and provide some mechanism by which officials can be reevaluated after their training.

So, the more things change the more they stay the change. An association can't empower potential leaders who aren't traditional association leaders until the association has its house in order.

When Group Leaders Disagree

The first thing group leaders have to do is define the conflict in understandable terms. What's the real problem? You need to define both the content issues and the relational issues. The content issues are those that are most obvious and what most of the squabbling is over, such as disagreement about your meeting formats or about how the association's money should be handled. The relational issues, on the other hand, are those issues involving personal feelings, biases and hidden agendas. Bottom line — you need to define the disagreement in specific terms that everyone involved can understand. So if two board members disagree on where a meeting should be held, examine the reason why meeting at a specific place is causing disagreement. Is the place itself the problem, which is a content issue, or do members feel they don't have a choice in choosing the place, which is a relational issue?

After defining the disagreement, leaders need to examine possible solutions. Brainstorm a list of possible solutions and write them all down. Then, the board as a group should rank them in order of most preferred to least preferred. It is extremely important to look for solutions that produce "win-win" situations. Try to avoid "win-lose" situations where one faction wins and the other faction loses. That will only create greater differences down the road.

The next thing you need to do is test possible solutions. See how everyone feels about it in the given moment and try to determine how others will feel in the days to follow. If you can agree that a solution looks good, then put it into actual practice and see how well it fairs. Study the various outcomes.

Next you must evaluate the solution. Did the tried solution rectify the disagreement or did it make things worse? Are the rewards and benefits of the solution evenly distributed? Are there other potential solutions that might be more effective?

At that point, you are going to accept or reject whatever it is you've tried to rectify the situation. If the solution worked, then the conflict was resolved and you will know what worked best for the next time. That will breed confidence in your association's leadership among the members of your association. If the solution failed, it's time to go back to your list of solutions and try something new.

Always remember two important facts about disagreements. First, within every problem lies a solution. That solution may not come quick and easy, but if worked on, it will eventually yield favorable results. Second, the only way to resolve any disagreement is to keep the lines of communication open no matter how disgruntled you become with the opposition. Being unwilling to talk things out will further hurt the potential to come to an amicable, positive resolution.

3

Critical Issues Confronting Leaders

In this chapter ...

- **Critical Challenges We Must Overcome Now**
  Eight of the most important issues impacting the officiating industry.

- **It's a Whole New Ballgame**
  The changing face of athletics and the expanded role officials are playing.

- **A View From the Top**
  Perspectives from seven high school athletic association leaders

Officiating leadership faces a host of challenges, and those challenges increase and change ever season. The more that athletics as a whole come under scrutiny, the more the officiating of those games comes under scrutiny. Leaders must face every challenge that arises head on and come to reasonable and innovative solutions.

In recent years such issues as poor sportsmanship, recruitment and retention of officials and accountability in officiating have impacted the officiating industry. Those challenges are part of the landscape and must be met every season, every game.

Critical Challenges We Must Overcome Now

Challenges are a part of life. How a person reacts to the challenges he or she is presented says a lot about that person.

What are some challenges officials face? Making correct calls? Getting proper angles? Being in the proper position? Yes, yes and yes. While those challenges present on the field and court are important, participants at the 2005 NASO Leadership Officiating Summit concentrated on broader challenges that face officials.

Jeffrey Stern, NASO staff member, introduced those challenges for discussion during a Summit session. The most critical included technology, rule enforcement, game management, public accountability, administrative support, reward structures, game security and recruitment and retention. Panelists Jerry Seeman, former senior NFL director of officiating; Anita Ortega, Division I women's basketball official; Jerry McGee, Division I football official and president of Wingate University, and Ronnie Carter, executive director of the Tennessee Secondary School Athletic Association, discussed the eight critical challenges facing officiating:

1. Technology — "The technology explosion is going to hit us all immediately," said Carter. "We're looking very closely at changing our whole concept of testing to where we would begin to test online, and use video training. The technology opportunities are going to explode before us and now we've got to figure out what we're going to do."

Ortega added, "Everything I do on my level is via the Internet. How many of you use computers? A show of hands. How many of you have BlackBerries? How many have iPods? That's the way we're going. And for those of you, the very small number, who are not on that boat, you're going to get left behind. Technology is here and it's going to get better, so that's the thing that we're going to have to really get a grip on."

McGee echoed those sentiments: "All correspondence now between the officials and the conference office is going to be via the computer. Our assignments must go out that way. Our game reports or foul reports, field judges do them and we do them every Sunday afternoon on the computer. Everything we're doing now touches technology. And if you aren't there you better get there as quickly as you can."

2. Administrative support — Officials hear time after time that administrators of officiating programs say officials are not valued. They are not understood and they're not valued. The panel looked at changing that culture.

"The concept of getting administrative support is not easy because we don't have control," said Carter. "One of the most interesting changes in officiating is this movement that when officials miss a critical judgment call in a big ballgame that has nationwide exposure, and then the next day you see in the paper that they've had two games removed from their schedule. We see that more now. That was unheard of 10 years ago. Now all of a sudden we see that. Where does that whole movement go? At the high school level we've never seen that as an option that we explore. We've never seen removing games from people for missing judgment calls. But that all plays into the area of administrative support. If officials at all levels don't have support then retention gets tougher and tougher no matter what we're coming up with as local leaders."

3. Game security — There is a lack of respect for officials and any kind of authority figure prevalent in our society today. One audience speaker related the following story that echoes the stories of many working officials: "One of the toughest challenges coming from baseball unfortunately is we're still changing in the parking lot. So unfortunately we've got to get undressed in the parking lot, but you're also right there when anybody wants to come by that's still upset about you banging the last guy out at the play to end the ballgame, then he's got to walk right by you to go to the car. The two, three or four officials, however many guys are on the game, you're out there by yourself so you've got to literally defend yourself. There's no security around. There's no administration from the schools even at the college level unfortunately."

4. Game management — It's a common scene in games these days: The official clearly warning a nearby coach or player that that's enough. Maybe he's putting up the "stop sign" with his hands. Maybe you can see him having a quiet word with the coach or player. But how effective are those warnings if there's never any follow through?

The panel discussed that whole concept of "managing a game" versus simply enforcing the rules. One audience speaker pointed out, "The primary role of an official is to manage the game. They're personnel managers and not just rules enforcers, and I think that game management skills are the things that keep everything flowing the right direction." The panel concluded that game management can be an effective tool when used prudently, but game management run amuck hurts the game, leading to the next critical issue:

5. Rule enforcement — "I have a love and desire for the rules, but I have a greater love and desire for the spirit and intent of the rules," said Seeman. "When you're working a game, no matter what it is, you're never out looking for things. You want the actions of the game to come to you. You sit back and watch: Is it within the spirit and intent of what it is? Yes, bingo. You're not going to be a great official by determining how many whistles you have or how many flags you throw or how many fouls are out there."

When a broad definition of elastic power extends into judgment, it's usually a case of officials interpreting the spirit and intent of a rule. In that sense, officials stretch the rules all the time, at all levels, in all sports. But that's not necessarily the intent of an elastic power clause. Most officiating programs teach the rulebook, but they also realize the intent of the rulebook is to provide advantage/disadvantage. To that end, officials don't always throw a flag when they spot holding. They certainly will when it affects the play. All its forms might not be completely spelled out in the rulebook, but defensive pass interference, for example, *is* in the rulebook, and it's the official's judgment that determines if it occurred. That's a matter of interpretation.

6. Public accountability — Scrutiny and accountability go hand in hand. The mission of the media is to report and comment on what happens in the games. The proliferation of the media leads to increased scrutiny. The more scrutiny there is, the more people will demand accountability. That accountability extends to everyone involved in athletic performance, from the players and coaches, to the league administrators and officials. Those other constituencies certainly have their share of mistakes during any given game. Ask media people and they'll tell you it's their right and duty to spread the word about deficiencies in officiating. Why is it the officials who most often get roasted in the media?

7. Recruitment and retention — "Certainly recruitment and retention is one of our biggest challenges," said Carter. "Even the people that we do get when they come right away if they don't get a varsity game in the second year then they're ready to leave. So it's really hard to keep them." The panel discussed how so many of the other critical challenges lead to recruitment and retention problems, such as the lack of adequate security and the intense public scrutiny on officials. "Those types of things," said Ortega, "don't make it very appealing for newer officials to want to stay."

8. Reward structures — The flip side of all that scrutiny and accountability that periodically leads to discipline is rewarding officials. Generally, officiating leaders don't consider rewards as much as discipline and that's problematic, according to the panel.

"I think we assume it takes a lot more to reward someone than it really does," said McGee. "A letter, phone call or e-mail when you see someone doing a great job officiating is all it takes. We need to spend more time rewarding people because we spend so much time on the negative."

Work done two years prior at the 2003 NASO Summit revealed the following list of officiating rewards:

> **More training for young officials:** Often, local associations don't have all the tools or finances at hand that are needed to properly train officials.

> **An open and fair evaluation system:** A common bone of contention for officials around the country, evaluation systems again came under scrutiny. Regularity, objectivity and responsiveness are all crucial issues that are often ignored.

> **Communication on number of games officials will receive:** In areas that use assigners, often new or younger officials don't have a clear idea of how they'll be scheduled going into a season. That makes it difficult to plan and train.

> **Accommodation of transferring officials:** An issue for some time, officials want to know that, if forced to move from state to state or even region to region within their state, they won't be forced to "the bottom of the ladder." Examples of former state championship officials being forced to work a JV schedule in their new state were plentiful.

> **Respect:** A broad issue that applies to every aspect of officiating.

> **More and better evaluations:** Evaluations once every few years simply aren't frequent enough. Also inadequate are evaluations that don't address all aspects of officiating.

> **More and better games:** Let's get rid of the "good 'ol boy networks" once and for all and be fair in assigning games.

▶ **More money:** Have game fees keep more in step with inflation and our costs.

▶ **Positive officiating environment:** Too often, officials have inadequate or even non-existent dressing facilities and other amenities. Baseball and softball umpires often have to dress in parking lots while trying not to be seen by passers-by.

▶ **A change in attitude:** So that officials are recognized as a vital part of the game by coaches, players, fans and administrators alike.

▶ **Communication, respect, support and feedback:** From all of those whom we serve.

▶ **To be treated as professionals:** Including understanding things from the officials' perspective.

▶ **Positive recognition:** At least from our local and state associations, but also from those outside those circles.

Both the panel and audience were also asked what they thought was missing from the critical list. Some suggestions included: defining the role of an official, sportsmanship, mentoring, time commitments, personal sacrifices and continuing education.

It's obvious that officials must face a lot, but what is the easiest challenge to fix? Seeman suggested "rule enforcement," if approached in the proper fashion. "Work with mentors and find out their experiences," said Seeman. "Know what's in the rulebook and casebook. When you put those together, that's where you can see people grow." Ortega voiced that fixing the reward structures would be the easiest. "How difficult is it to pat someone on the back? I think out of those eight challenges, reward structures are something that can be resolved," she said.

While solutions may be in sight for some of the eight, others look to have a longer life. Which of the challenges is here to stay? While technology, and its use in officiating, will continue to grow,

Carter had a unique view about the challenge of recruiting and retention.

"No one will ever have an overabundance of good officials," he said. "Even if you have more warm bodies, you'll always be looking for good officials. You have to make a concerted effort to recruit officials to replace those who have moved up."

It seems some, if not all, of the eight challenges will continue to be addressed for years to come. How individuals react to those challenges will help shape the industry.

It's a Whole New Ballgame

Other aspects of the game have also changed how officials officiate and the expectations officiating leaders have for the men and women working in the trenches.

It's no secret that officials are taking on more responsibility with each passing season. No longer is officiating a game your weekly bit of community service with some money thrown in. It's become an ever more time consuming avocation demanding levels of fitness, intelligence and leadership that the people who used to officiate the games never had to deal with.

In addition to calling plays that happen in the game, officials are doing so many more things than they did a generation ago. They are fashion police, on the prowl for this week's theme bracelet and dangling shirttails. If there's lightning around, the referee is the storm center anchor. So that we don't miss the fun of a pregame rumble, we're cops walking the beat for up to an hour beforehand … just in case. Why are officials getting all that foisted upon them? Well, there are a lot of reasons, but Big 12 football referee John Bible boils it down to three.

"Number one," says Bible, "is situations." We are popular assignees of corrective action for past calamities. In fact, Bible was at the center of one of those events. His football crew once stood by and watched a full-scale donnybrook between the teams before a game started because the rules gave them no jurisdiction until the coin toss. After the incident, that all changed and officials were required to be present long before the game started. Often, as he says, responsibilities are added as a reaction to events.

Abdication is the second reason why officials get more workload, says Bible. "If the coaches wanted the socks up and the pads in, all they'd have to do is tell their kids to get the socks up and pads in," he reasons. "But it's kind of hard for Charley Coach to tell Sammy Stud Quarterback, 'Get yourself proper,' so it falls on us." Officials tend to get some responsibility out of convenience; they're there anyway and nobody else wants to deal with what must be dealt with.

Third, and the motivation that seems to get the most sympathy from officials, is the risk of litigation. Bible, an attorney, says, "We live in a litigious society. The plaintiff's attorneys — and I've been one — take the shotgun approach: If somebody gets hurt, you sue everybody and his kid sister, because if I sue eight different defendants and seven of them don't have the assets, I can get it out of the eighth dude and guess what? I'm happy." So, as officials, we're being given an active role in making sure that ambulance chasers never get the chance. We're in the best position to be the gatekeepers of risk management.

Those topics were discussed in-depth during a Summit session titled, "A Whole New Ballgame: The Expanding Responsibilities of Sports Officials." Panelists Bible, major college men's basketball assigner Dale Kelley, *Referee* Publisher Barry Mano, NFL Director of Officiating Mike Periera and NFHS Assistant Executive Director Mary Struckhoff talked about why officials are being saddled with such duties and what the new reality means to the men and women working the games, who often aren't enamored with the expanded roles.

The New Reality

Pereira had some advice for those not interested in expanded duties, which could be summarized in one word: Quit. "You know what," says Pereira, "That's life. There are more and more responsibilities put on us at all levels whether it's our regular job or our avocation here.

"We have to learn how to accept them and really learn how to turn them into a positive." Pereira said that officials, whether they're the 120 pro-level guys on his staff or the kid umpiring a T-ball game, have to understand that they share the responsibility with the teams and spectators of "presenting a game *and* a product." And that appears to be the rub. Some officials would prefer to breeze in, call all the plays and slip out without getting any of the product on them. But their role is now very much one of taking *leadership* in protecting the trademark. Sorry, Charlie, leagues want officials to be where the buck stops.

Kelley, an NCAA men's basketball assigner for five Division I conferences, agrees with that attitude. He said today's official has to take the approach that, "… This is *my* game. It's our responsibility and we've accepted that obligation and responsibility" to enforce the rules as they're given, not as we'd like them to be. He and others believe that the best officials, among other things, renounce their own feelings and opinions of what they *should* be doing when they step on the court. From that point, it's no longer about them but about the game.

Mano, an outspoken advocate for the officiating profession, likened that notion to how the police work. "I like to say that we're in the enforcement division," he said. "We're not in the legislative division, so the things we do basically are responsive or reactive to what comes down from the legislative division." OK, so officiating coordinators like Pereira and Kelley can find enough referees willing to do what they're told, who can holster their personal opinions in favor of some notoriety and big game fees. But what about the rest of us who feel like we're getting to be the sump pump for every little whim that crosses a rules committee's mind? Certainly, a school assistant with a clipboard and a pair of binoculars could handle uniform infractions. Maybe a guy with a kite and a key could help decide when the lightning's too close. And how about actually having someone with even a little medical training make a determination of whether a kid was unconscious? Why does it always have to be the officials?

The Last Line of Defense

Struckhoff pointed one compelling reason: "Funny enough, but a lot of rule changes and situations unfortunately happen because coaches don't trust one another," she said. "That's one of the reasons officials have the responsibilities they do and why in some cases those responsibilities are growing. It's because coaches don't trust each other but they do trust us. So whether we like it or not, that's a good statement they're making. But it does tend to lead us into more responsibilities over time."

An A.D. (of the losing team) halting a game for approaching lightning may not get the same benefit of the doubt as the referee. But when it comes to unfounded suspicions of homerism, officials are often on the receiving end of that, too — what makes them a *better* choice? Pereira believes you can't be distracted by the outliers, and uses some personal experience in support.

Pereira was called into jury duty on a civil case and the attorneys of the plaintiff and defendant were examining potential panelists about their fitness to serve. "They were questioning all 30 of the jurors with, 'What's your occupation?' 'Could you award a million dollars to a person?' 'Can you do this?'" began Pereira. "Then they came to me and they never asked me a question — not the defendant's nor the plaintiff's attorney. I thought, 'This is good. I'm not going to be on the jury.' But I was the first person selected.

"I asked them afterward why they would pick me without asking any questions and they said, 'From the nature of your job, we figured you would be impartial.' Interestingly enough, that's the feeling everybody has about officials, which hopefully is true."

Where Does It End?

You don't have to be impartial to judge uniform requirements, merely sighted. That's true but more than that is needed. For example, a high school track team in California was recently disqualified from a meet because one of its members had a string tied around her ankle. Jewelry, you know. A meet official made that call, but how much more often would it happen if we sloughed off those decisions on someone who didn't have our training and experience? The referees might not always have the wherewithal, but the odds strongly favor them.

Some chores may be a little excessive as Bible agrees but, with an increasing workload placed on officials, there's also another important trend. It's greater representation of officials on rules and competition committees at all levels. Most of the major sports do that. OK, the referees in the room aren't usually allowed an actual vote but, by-and-large, their advice on the technical issues of implementing rule and procedure changes is heeded. That makes it likely that jobs assigned to officials have been thought out from everyone's standpoint, so we're best off to get on with life and just do them. But isn't the hassle for officials likely to grow as the lawyers get more imaginative?

Pereira thinks it'll be just the opposite. He sees that professional and collegiate sports are taking a more proactive approach to potential problems. In other words, the pattern is changing from one of reaction to problems to planning for what could happen and thereby blunting the effect when they actually do occur. He admits that you can never fully expect the unexpected but says that his league and others have developed procedures for handling many events that could conceivably affect a game. That way, the role of the officials is best respected. In the NFL, for instance, a policy manual explains exactly what decisions are in the hands of the officials and what steps are to be taken in various emergencies. Then the NFL relies on its officials to know the procedures, follow them and use common sense about anything else. It's all about risk minimization and it is imperative for officials to be the poster children for seeing things are done the right way.

When you think about it, having more to do as officials is a good bit better than having less. What would it say if referees were actually being marginalized? After all, at the office, most of us would like to be regarded as indispensable because it makes us harder to get rid of. Wishing we had more to do at work would be a sure sign of trouble brewing.

A View From the Top

As the culture of athletics continues to change and officials and officiating leaders meet new and sometimes unwelcome challenges, they can take some solace knowing that others in the athletic community are concerned, too.

The majority of officials in this country work high school sports, and it's at that level of competition that the major issues facing officials are most critical. NASO sat down with the heads of seven state high school associations to discuss the critical issues facing prep officials and glean some insight into what those at that level are doing on behalf of the officials.

The Biggest Concern

NASO: When it comes to officiating, what keeps you up at night?

Marty Hickman: It's definitely numbers. There are times that I wonder whether or not we're really going to have enough officials to keep some of our programs running. We could lose our boys' gymnastics program because we don't have enough officials.

Ronnie Carter: Literally nothing keeps me up at night about officiating. But that having been said, the biggest concern with me involves the personnel who are leading our officials' groups. Our whole officiating program is based so much on our local associations. Everything is dependent on the strength of the leaders we have at the trench level. Who's going to take the next person's place leading a particular group?

State Association Executive Directors' Round Table

During the 2005 Summit, NASO sat down with the heads of seven state high school association executive directors.

While some have officiating experience in their backgrounds, those seven men have a perspective different from officials or officiating supervisors because they are charged with the oversight of the entire high school athletic experience.

Ronnie Carter

Carter is the executive director of the Tennessee Secondary School Athletic Association. His career has been spent in secondary education as a teacher, coach, official and administrator for the past 36 years. Carter has served on the NFHS basketball and football rules committees. He currently serves on the NASO board of directors and is a past president of the NFHS board of directors.

Doug Chickering

Chickering began his career as a teacher-coach and later was a principal, athletic director and a district administrator. He became the Wisconsin Interscholastic Athletic Association executive director in 1986. Chickering earned a master's degree in school administration from the University of Wisconsin-Superior in 1971.

Evan Excell

Excell has been the executive director of the Utah High School Activities Association since 1994. Prior to that, he was a teacher, coach and athletic director for 28 years. He received his bachelor's degree in physical education and his master's degree in educational administration from the University of Utah.

Ron Laird: Our concern is also numbers. Our first week of playoffs we actually don't have enough football crews to cover all of our games. We have to double some games and have crews do two games to cover them.

Ralph Swearngin: Knock on wood, fortunately we've had 10 straight years of registration growth, so numbers aren't our particular problem across the board. What we're really struggling with right now is we're trying to get our schools out of paying travel wages. It's very difficult for our athletic directors to budget effectively, so we're trying to find a magic formula to increase our game fees enough to bring in the right average so that one game you may have to travel a long way, but the next one may be in your backyard and you'll be OK.

Doug Chickering: A concern that we continually address as a staff has to do with the selection and assignment of officials for postseason play. There are always allegations about politics, about favoritism. We don't assign officials during the regular season, but we do all of the assignments during the postseason, so we've been struggling with that for three or four years and can't seem to find any one way of doing it that makes officials feel appreciated. We've

Marty Hickman

Hickman joined the Illinois High School Association staff in 1991 as an assistant director and then associate director. He became the executive director in 2001. He received his doctorate in education from the University of Illinois at Champaign-Urbana. Hickman has served on the NFHS's Strategic Planning Team, Citizenship Committee and basketball rules committee.

Jerry Hughes

Hughes has been the executive director of the Nevada Interscholastic Activities Association since 1989. Prior to that, he was a high school district athletic director and coach. Hughes received his bachelor's degree from Adams State College in Colorado. He officiated high school football, basketball, baseball and softball for eight years in the 1970s.

Ron Laird

Laird became Commissioner of the Wyoming High School Activities Association in 2004, after 26 years as a teacher, coach, assistant principal and activities director. He received his bachelor's degree from Eastern Montana College and a master's from the United States Sports Academy in Daphne, Ala.

Ralph Swearngin

Swearngin has been with the Georgia High School Association since 1992. Prior to that, Swearngin was a professor and basketball and baseball coach for 20 years at Atlanta Christian College in East Point, Ga. He had been a high school football official in Georgia and California for 22 years. Swearngin has served on the NFHS football and softball rules committees.

had ad hoc committees discussing it. One message I've heard from officiating representatives on those committees is that officials were born to bitch.

NASO: We're all laughing at that, but is there some truth in that statement?

Chickering: In that regard, yes. The week before our state basketball tournament perhaps more than anything else, before the officials are assigned, the people who think they ought to be there will start calling the people in our office who do the assigning, and they'll have all of these unusual situations that have occurred and how they've dealt with them. Of course they know the way they dealt with them was right but they sure want to get their message before the group. We might see some relief from that now that we're going to three-person crews for our basketball tournament series. We hope that we'll get some of the young people who want to officiate to get games so they will stay in officiating.

Jerry Hughes: With our population growth in Nevada, we're struggling with keeping up the numbers of officials. We just have constant problems with that. But we keep looking for solutions. On the way over here I wrote a memo to our schools and asked each school in Nevada to recruit a male and a female official, students who had been good athletes who might make good judgments, those kind of kids. Some of our leagues have to adjust their schedules because of the officiating numbers. Instead of playing Friday night football, we'll have Thursday and Saturday games because there are not enough crews to cover all games on one night. Basketball is the same way. We're in a crisis really.

Recruitment and Retention

NASO: Officiating shortages obviously are a big problem and Jerry mentioned some actions his office is taking. What else can a state association do to address the problem of recruiting and retaining officials? Ralph, you said Georgia has experienced 10 years of growth. How have you done that?

Swearngin: We're doing a couple of things. We built into our TV contract public service announcements to feature officials. That's one small thing, but our best approach is utilizing satisfied customers. What I mean by that is if you've got officials who enjoy officiating, they are the best people to bring in other people. The big hurdle is we have to get over the mentality some officials have that every new official means competition for games. We have to make them see that growth in the profession is good for everybody.

We're trying to find ways to break up some of the fiefdoms, the kingdoms that have developed over time. We're doing that by having the associations share training and share officials with each other. That dilutes the political networks a little bit and deserving officials who are not part of the old boy network get a better chance to work and will stay on board as officials instead of leaving because they can't get games. When we find an official who looks good and that official's name doesn't appear on a (postseason) nomination list from an association, we write a letter back to the association: "We saw this official; what a great official. We certainly hope that we're going to be seeing his name on your lists in times to come." That puts pressure back on them.

Carter: I don't mean to minimize our role because I understand the state association has a role, but it's minor as compared to where the real recruiting of officials has got to take place — at the local level. It has to take place in the trenches, and for us, that's where we lean so heavily on our local leaders.

NASO: How do you encourage them to be more active?

Carter: We have trainers, or supervisors we call them, in all of our local associations. We bring those people to our office every year prior to that sport season. They spend a day with our staff members going over rule changes, points of emphasis and sharing concerns and information with each other from all over our state. From that, we're seeing that they realize they need to recruit and it has to be a concerted effort. What we have found over the course of time is the worst recruiters of officials are school people. It would be logical that you do what Jerry said, but our experience in that has been our coaches, who ought to be the best, are the worst. The people who recruit officials best are other officials.

Hickman: What we've tried to do in that regard is just cultivate those relationships with associations. We do some of the things that Ronnie talked about, we bring them in, plus we do a lot of going out on the road to association meetings with people from our staff, and then last year we provided some grant money to associations to develop recruiting materials. We have an application process, and have a pool of money where associations can get up to $500 a year to develop recruiting programs. That's worked out well. And we have seen our numbers increase — not quite as dramatically as Ralph's increases, but over the last five years we've had fairly steady increases in our officials licenses.

Officials Strengths and Weaknesses

NASO: Talking about relying so heavily on the officials in the trenches, what's your opinion of the regular Joe referees? What would each of you consider the greatest strengths and weaknesses of the officials in your state?

Hickman: Their passion for the games and their desire to give back to young people is an incredible strength. On the other hand, at times they're awfully hard on themselves. We'll have a number of officials who will beat themselves up over mistakes from time to time, and mistakes happen in life and in contests.

Carter: The bond that develops and the relationships are impressive. I think that's the greatest strength officials have. As for a weakness, it's probably the inability to see the bigger picture sometimes. Our older guys used to just pound the rulebook and the casebook. We don't see that commitment to rules knowledge as much. It's just, "Give me a little bit of a base and let me have a game."

Hughes: Our strength in Nevada right now is the officiating leadership we have. We have some really excellent leaders who do a good job. As for a weakness, it's got to be that officials seem very clique-ish. There are only three people who are going to work a state championship game, and 100 who think it ought to be them. They're difficult sometimes on each other.

Excell: Our strength comes from a rather small group of leaders who carry the load for officiating in the state. Our concern is that they're getting older. It doesn't seem like we're getting the leadership and dedication from the group that's coming up, so I'm concerned about that. One weakness that nobody's mentioned, and it's getting to be a problem, is the little chit-chattiness of the officials out there. We can talk about coaches chirping at officials. We have the same problem in reverse. We have officials chirping at coaches, and little chit-chats that go on. That's only a small group, but that's probably as big a weakness as we have.

Laird: We started some mechanics camps and training and we've got a lot of officials who want to get better. That is a real strength, the people wanting to learn and get better. I think probably the weakness is some of those guys have a tendency to not look at themselves in terms of how they can get better. They worry more about what others are doing. Who's getting the games and how can they put their names out front.

Swearngin: Our strength is in our training programs and the officials' response to them. Our prepared materials, our camps and clinics — those are very strong. Probably our biggest weakness has to be the attitude of the officials. It's kind of ironic, whenever people are evaluated and scored on subjective things, there's just always an uneasiness about it. Officials are athletes for the most part, and there's a competitive aspect to what they do. Yet the very nature of the job is about impartiality, harnessing your ego. That produces some inner tensions, so they take it out on each other. They see each other as competitors instead of compatriots.

Chickering: Our strengths are commitment, passion, willingness to accept changes in mechanics and number of people on crews and all those things our officials have bought into. I've been in this business now for 20 years and we've always worried as each generation of people leave that we're losing our leadership. Who's going to replace that person within the ranks of the officials? But new leaders always emerge. If there's a weakness universally among the officials of all abilities, I think it is their inability to admit, even to themselves, that they may have made a mistake. They don't have to get on a soapbox and tell the world that they blew a call, but they can make life a lot easier for themselves, and for our office, too, if they would acknowledge that maybe that call was wrong and not be quite so critical of us or of their partners or other people within their associations for not supporting them to the Nth degree.

Sportsmanship

NASO: Poor sportsmanship is another issue that's a hot topic among officials. Evan, you recently dealt with a sportsmanship issue in your state, didn't you?

Excell: We did. We had four incidents that were pretty bad, and they were all with coaches and coach-official relationships. Our board just said, "We've had enough of this; we're going to haul those schools and coaches in, conduct hearings on this and come up with some penalties." So we did. In one of the cases, the girls' basketball team that was expected to win our state tournament got beat in the finals. We have a corporate-sponsored trophy presentation and the girls wouldn't come out to accept the second-place trophy. One of the players said, "Just put it on the floor." We had some coaches verbally attack me and others in our office after a double overtime loss. In another one, one of our hall of fame coaches — a gentleman with a whole bunch of state championships — left a voice mail for me telling us how corrupt we were and how we stacked the odds against them in assigning officials and they lost in the quarterfinals. The end result of all that is our board came down pretty hard for us with fines, penalties. That hall of fame coach misses the first five games of the girls' basketball season this year, a $1,000 fine, probation and a letter of reprimand. The other coaches paid a $750 fine and received probation, and the girls' basketball team got a $500 fine and probation. We're hoping the message is out there.

Hughes: We're attempting to get our officials more involved with our sportsmanship program. We feel that's one of the weak areas we have. We have one coach — like I'm sure everybody in this room has — where all the officials say, "When are you going to do something about this guy?" I had a personal meeting with him. I said, "Look, we need some help from you. Certain people look up to you; you have a good program." He says, "I have one question: If everybody thinks I'm so bad, why have I not received a technical foul in two years?" Now I don't have a leg to stand on for the officials. I have to take that back to the officials association and say, "You know what? You guys have to enforce the rules." We're planning a major sportsmanship emphasis in basketball this year and we're looking to our officials to really support our current sportsmanship program by enforcing the rules as they're written, not letting it slide.

Laird: We've put in what we call a "buy back" program in which if a coach is ejected or a player is ejected, they've got to go through a class before they'll be allowed to participate again. That's been a pretty good deterrent. We have more coach ejections in soccer than any other sport, and this last spring we had zero ejections on the season for the first time. If they're ejected, they actually have to go through a full class and take a test, watch a video and those types of things before they're allowed to participate again.

Technology in Officiating

NASO: With the Internet making communication so easy and the advent of online testing, registration and training, technology in officiating is all the rage. What are your state offices utilizing in terms of technology for officials?

Hickman: We've done a number of things. We issue a lot of our contracts online now. We do our availability for our state tournament series online. Our ratings system is all online, and we're just coming out with an interactive education program. Eventually it'll be on our website. It's out now in DVD form, but it's an interactive education program that deals with all kinds of plays and mechanics in virtually all of our activities. (IHSA Assistant Executive Director) Dave Gannaway spent hour after hour looking at footage and then sat down with our head clinicians and picked out the best teaching examples. You can go on and click a series of plays under a number of topics and then go through each of those. Sometimes you get a chance to put in your judgment as to what you think the call should be before you know what the call is on the play. It should be a really good thing. It's not quite complete, but it's real close.

Carter: We're doing very little right now, but we've already announced we're looking at major changes that will start as early as '06-'07, and the first one is getting our testing program online; we're changing our whole testing thought process and format. And we will be stealing all of Illinois' stuff (laughs). As always about three-fourths of the stuff we do in Tennessee, we steal from Illinois.

Hickman: Really, it doesn't make any sense for, at least in my view, another state's staff to sit down and do the same thing that we've just done. In this particular instance we may be out in front. That's great, but we're happy to share that with the rest of the country, because we'll end up looking for help from Wisconsin or Tennessee or whoever on some other issue down the road.

Laird: We've used our website with our officials mostly as a communication tool. But all of our rules clinics are over a video conference. Each high school in the state has a video conference site. We went to that out of necessity because of the great distances between our officials, and between our schools for that matter.

Chickering: We have a password-protected official center on our website and we do some levels of our testing in that. Every year we add a thing or two to the officials' center. Initially, we had some concerns about all officials not having access to the technology to use it, but that has not proven to be a real problem.

Swearngin: We're a little bit behind on the technology curve. We have a website, and we don't keep it up like we ought to. We've done some videos, taking film clips, especially basketball and use those in our summer camps and in our pre-tournament clinic that we have for all the officials selected to work. We've done some graphics on computers with mechanics in football, demonstrating where people move. We're in about the second year of that. We'd like to put our testing online, but we're going to wait and let the other states work the bugs out of it before we head in that direction.

4

Leadership
Resources

The 2005 NASO Summit featured a mini-seminar in the "Art of Verbal Judo" by Dr. George Thompson, the program's founder and president. While not an official himself, Thompson's program is widely used in professions such as law enforcement, teaching and other endeavors in which verbal conflicts are likely.

Thompson's program has practical applications to very specific instances when a coach or other game participant verbally confronts officials.

Additionally, Summit keynote speaker Ed T. Rush, retired NBA director officiating, offered his take on leadership based in part on the philosophies of leadership guru and author John Maxwell. In 2002 Maxwell discussed leadership principles in regard to officiating with NASO and his perspective is included in this chapter.

The Art of Verbal Judo

Verbal Judo, or tactical communications, is the gentle art of persuasion that redirects others' behavior with words and generates voluntary compliance. Thompson presented his program in short form at the NASO Summit.

Verbal Judo is a system of expression designed to defuse animosities. Its methods embrace the notion that one must subdue natural impulses in dealing with antagonists, because the basic human inclination is to fight back verbally when challenged or insulted. Therefore, Verbal Judo is a learned response, and its success can be measured by the amount of ingrained tendencies a person is able to overcome. In other words, what comes naturally can come harmfully. Sports officials must sublimate their natural human reactions in verbal confrontations.

Thompson maintains that "the cocked tongue" is the most dangerous weapon in tense situations today. The impetus for firing off retaliatory, caustic rejoinders has to be muffled if a person in charge of soliciting cooperation from others is to influence people successfully. "The ultimate goal is voluntary compliance," Thompson says, and for the most part he is speaking of society's rules enforcers such as airline flight attendants, hospital emergency room nurses, recreational directors, police officers, sports officials and even nightclub bouncers and parking lot personnel.

How would it work for sports officials? Well, to understate it, sometimes officials find themselves in a hostile environment. When the going gets tough, the human reaction is to dig in your heels and offer firm resistance. Wrong move, Thompson says. The ordinary habit of aggressive reaction has to be replaced by a transformed method of studied response. Studied because verbal judo is an acquired skill; it does not flow instinctively.

Don't be confused by the name. Although judo is indeed a martial art, it is a *defensive* strategy. Karate is the aggressive Japanese form of combat. Judo seeks to deflect the thrust of an attacker and use that force to affect a beneficial result. Hence, verbal judo is strictly a defense mechanism, what could be called parrying. "Judo is the art of redirecting an opponent's energy to achieve a goal," is how Thompson phrases it.

The first requisite for easing a tense verbal encounter is actually two-pronged. First, Thompson says, you must "learn to take crap with dignity and style." Second, you must learn to project empathy. Empathy is not the same as sympathy. You don't have to feel the other person's pain, but you do have to step into his shoes — or his head — figuratively, understanding exactly what his motivation may be and acknowledging that motivation by projecting a clear show of respect. Thompson says that carries with it a commitment to partnership. "We're in this thing together. Let's move toward a goal of reasonable harmony. The integrity of the game is what's important."

Dr. George Thompson

Dr. George Thompson is the president and founder of the Verbal Judo Institute, a tactical training and management firm based in Auburn, N.Y. Thompson has an eclectic background, having taught English on the high school level, English Literature on the university level and served as a full- and part-time police officer. Also a martial artist, he holds black belts in Judo and Taekwondo. Dr. Thompson has written four books on Verbal Judo, each analyzing ways to defuse conflict and redirect behavior into more positive channels. Thompson received his B.A. from Colgate University (1963), his Masters' and Doctorate in English from the University of Connecticut (1972), and he completed post-doctoral work at Princeton University in Rhetoric and Persuasion (1979). Widely published in magazines and periodicals, his training has been highlighted nationally on NBC, ABC and CBS News, CNN, *48 Hours, Inside Edition, In the Line of Duty*, and Fox News, as well as in the *Los Angeles Times, N.Y. Post, Sacramento Bee* and other publications.

Dealing With Difficult People

Thompson told the Summit attendees that there are five steps to take when you're dealing with a difficult person:

1. Ask for cooperation. "You can either ask someone for their cooperation or tell them you're going to get their cooperation," said Thompson. "It's much better to ask; it soothes them, helps disarm them."

2. Set the context. "Tell them why you're talking to them," Thompson said. "Say, 'Would you come over here a minute. Let me tell you why I need to talk to you.' You set the context. When you set context, 70 percent or more of the people will do what you want them to do because you've explained yourself, showed them respect. Everybody thinks they deserve to know something. Don't tell people to do stuff without telling them why. A lot of people think telling people why is weak. It's actually extremely strong. Let me tell you why. Let me tell you why I made that call. Let me tell you why this man is being ejected from the game. I'll be glad to tell you."

3. Give them options. "How do you present options to a man or woman?" Thompson asked. "There are three tricks to it:

"1. The voice has to sound like you care that he takes the good option.

"2. Options put positives first, negatives second, which is not natural. It's natural for a referee to say, 'You want to be thrown out of the game?' Never do that. Never put the negative first. Put the positive options, because if you put the negative first, the fight is on. Positive softens them up, calms them down. They like that because it's in their best interest.

"3. The third secret of options is to be specific. Don't say, 'You'll be in trouble.' It's too vague. Describe the trouble. 'Let me tell you what's going to happen if you continue to yell. You will be ejected from the game. You know what that means? That means this guy that you don't think is very good who is your assistant coach is going to run this team in this crucial game. So why don't you just smile as if we both have agreed that both of us are right, and go sit down.'"

4. Confirm their option. "That is the ultimate nicety," Thompson explained. "Let's say the coach says, 'I'm not stepping off the field.' You say, 'Is there anything that I could say at this time or my colleagues could say at this time to get you to step back on the sidelines so we can proceed with this game as we both, I would like to think, would want to? Is there anything I could say, sir, to get you to do that? I'd like to think so.'"

5. Act. "If the answer to your question in step four is no," said Thompson, "he's gone.

"Now any official can go back to his or her boss or supervisor, whoever asks and completely defend the action. 'Look, I asked if words would work and he said no.' Notice how much stronger the position of the official is. 'I didn't just toss him out because I got angry. I asked him would words work and he said no, so in the interest of the game and the interest of the fans, that man had to be taken off.' I need to act in such a way that you can defend me. If I use profanity — Get the F out of here! — and that's complained about, I don't give my boss any grounds to defend me. How do you defend a guy who can't control his tongue? You can't."

How to Control Your Own Tongue

"Treat people with respect simply because it's right," is Thompson's simple credo. To be a judicious responder you have to contrive substitute words for expressions that may come readily to your lips. According to Thompson, you have to put a silencer on the cocked tongue by:

a. Using words to redirect the negative force of others.

b. Practicing mind-mouth harmony.

c. Taking control of situations without escalating stress and frustration.

Before explaining what phrases make verbal judo work, Thompson offers some caveats. Patent reactions that antagonize rather than empathize include:

"That's the rule." Hiding behind a formal definition just throws up a smokescreen, according to the author. "Rather," he says, "Explain your purpose, pointedly, briefly, using logic to clarify." Officials are sometimes inclined to illustrate their knowledge by offering rulebook definitions in support of decisions. If judgment is based on a rule interpretation, the way to explain it is to use "game" language and condense the concept in a one or two sentence overview.

"Calm down." That phrase works just the opposite. It infuriates. Instead settle for, "Let's talk. What's the trouble?" Get an explanation, because explaining defuses anger. A critical strategy for officials when challenged or attacked is to turn the situation into a listening encounter. Easy to say, hard to do. But the longer a person talks, the less fervid his animosity is. The official must stifle the urge for a blunt reaction. A judicious pause may be the most effective communication device there is. A docile countenance can also beget a mellower approach.

"Be reasonable." The only way to stimulate rationality is to be reasonable yourself. You can deflect unreasoning by paraphrasing what you heard. After listening, "report back" to the speaker. "Here's what I heard you say" works better than an outright denial of the other person's position. After the paraphrase an official may relay his point effectively through a frank issuance of logic. That assures that the antagonist's point has been heard, digested and addressed.

Nice Guys, Wimps and Difficult People

Thompson divides people into three categories: Nice People, Wimps and Difficult People. Nice People are generally pretty easy to deal with. Contrary to what the name usually conjures, Wimps aren't really pushovers. They'll back off but will look for a chance to get you later. They have to be confronted and dealt with forthrightly.

"Difficult People insist on causal explanations. They want to know *why* — all the time. 'Why' is the bottom line in America. It is the essence of a *can do* culture, one that bulldozes obstacles," Thompson said. Coaches in combat are usually Difficult People. They want to know why judgments have been made. They aren't interested in a level playing field. They're determined to be mavericks, to succeed on their own terms. As we all know, they can be annoyingly persistent, goading in their queries and assertions.

It's possible a person can be all three types given the circumstances. You choose your own role, most of the time. Sometimes you'll back off, sometimes you'll be feisty, and sometimes you'll be nice, depending on how you ascertain the rewards. "How can I best win" is the game.

The 14 Benefits of Paraphrasing

"To paraphrase, put most simply, is to put another person's meaning into words and deliver it back to him," said Thompson. "If you're taking abuse, you want to somehow intrude so you can make the diatribe a conversation. Then you can cast what you think lies behind his aggressive words (his real point) in your own words (which will be calmer because you're not the emotionally charged one here), and be sure that you have heard it correctly."

When done correctly, you can reap the following benefits:

1. The other person is obliged to listen.
2. You've taken control.
3. You're verifying your own perceptions.
4. Thus, you can be corrected.
5. You make the other person a better listener.
6. You've created empathy yourself.
7. You've gained attention.
8. You've identified "sonic intention" (a person thought he said something he really didn't say).
9. You've clarified for bystanders (assistants, players, possibly spectators).
10. It prevents "metaphrasing" (putting words in others' mouths).
11. It promotes "reverse" paraphrasing (whereby the other person paraphrases you).
12. It allows for "rephrasing" (a beneficial, problem-solving dialogue).
13. It generates a "fair play" response (it forces the other person to play by your rules).
14. It etches facts in your own mind.

Using Verbal Judo in Officiating

Here are some specific situations you may be familiar with: A baseball coach comes down from the coaching box at the end of an inning, on the way to the players' bench. He stops and speaks in even tones: "It looks to me like you're calling shoulder-high pitches strikes. I can see the level from where I stand. My catcher also says some of the strikes you're calling are unhittable." OK, there's the needle. How do you extract it?

How about this one from the football field: "You know that punter took a dive! My man barely breathed on him. C'mon, everything's going their way. All you've got is a fistful of flags for us. You're terrible!"

Or this one from the basketball court: "You know darned well their player knocked that ball out of bounds. What're you looking at? Besides, their pivot guy is camped in the lane. Can't you count to three seconds? I'm tired of your gnawing on that whistle! You guys reek. We get a hose job every time we come here."

How can you really "take crap with dignity" as Thompson teaches? That is a psychological mindset. Good officials can program themselves to shuck verbal slings and arrows. That means letting a person have a full say without flinching. Then start by acknowledging that a person may have a legitimate point of view (empathy), even if he doesn't have one. Thompson offers catchphrases, such as, "I appreciate that, I see your point, you're entitled to that view, I hear you, that may well be, I understand that, etc." All of those catchphrases are then followed by the word *but* …. Then the response follows, delivered with a modulated voice pitch, measured pace and even tone.

If things are more heated, you may need to immediately take control of the conversation by beginning with a phrase like, "Whoa! Hold on. Wait a sec." Those additional "strip phrases," as Thompson calls them, are the springboards for the parrying process. "Let's be sure I heard you right," is the next step, which also shows you're empathizing with the other person. Then follows the genuine secret of the judo act, *paraphrasing* (see sidebar). Keep in mind, as Thompson said, that "90 percent of your success will lie in your delivery style."

"Remember," Thompson said, "you are on display. Your uniform and your position guarantee that. (You also possess the *hammer*, but you don't have to use it.) Consequently, you are an actor. … In some sense you have to put on a show. You don't have to save face." But the other person may indeed have to save face: before his players, in the eyes of his assistants, in the regard of his other followers. He has constituents; you do not.

To some degree, Thompson said, you have to "train yourself to say the opposite of what you feel" when under verbal attack. You have to "use language disinterestedly, unemotionally and without bias." It is not acceptable for the official to fight back. If you do blurt a sharp commentary, what may make you feel good temporarily is likely to make you feel bad in the long run.

For more information on Dr. Thompson's Verbal Judo program and his books, *Verbal Judo: The Gentle Art of Persuasion*, *Verbal Judo: Redirecting Behavior With Words* and *Verbal judo: Words as a Force Option*, please go to www.verbaljudo.com.

Indispensable Qualities of a Leader

Rush often used Maxwell's books, most notably *21 Indispensable Qualities of a Leader,* in officiating training while he was director of NBA officiating, and had Maxwell speak at preseason camps. In 2002, Maxwell discussed leadership in relation to sports officials with NASO:

NASO: Do officials need to be leaders?

Maxwell: Absolutely. They are leaders. There are two camps about leadership. One is leading by position — the person who puts on the uniform, gets the whistle and says, "I'm the referee. I'm the final say." There's another camp that says you lead by influence. The only way you can do that is by being good with relationships. You can't influence people positively if you can't relate to them in a positive way. Referees have a unique role. A leader normally gets to have momentum on his or her side — things are going good and everybody is happy to follow the leader. But every time you blow the whistle, you're going to make somebody unhappy. You're doing exactly opposite of a leader. Instead of giving permission and empowering, you're stopping. So your leadership is much more difficult. But you're not looking to provide happiness, you're looking for a common ground of respect. You can blow the whistle on somebody and if they respect you, they'll be fine.

NASO: How can referees obtain that leadership based on common ground?

Maxwell: It's reached when both coaches walk off the floor, look at you and identify when you called a good game, because you have their respect. Common ground occurs when you make a decision that people do not care for but you've listened to them, and can understand why they think the way they do. For example, you might say, "You just have to understand I'm going to make a decision that you're not going to care for, but if I were sitting where you are, I'd be shooting for the same thing as you." That's the common ground that you're looking for in identification. Your goal is not to make both coaches happy, but your goal is to identify with each other. You still made the call and, so you didn't please them, but you have their respect.

NASO: How do referees identify with players?

Maxwell: If you're seeing teams on a continual basis, like in the NBA, as a leader you must know the temperament of the players. At the high school level, I think you identify by making the calls in an instructive and constructive way. When I played at the high school level, I had many refs before making a call on me come over and say, "You're getting in the lane; your left foot is sliding in there. Watch your foot." What they really did is say, "If you don't move your left foot this next time before the guy shoots, you're going to get this call on you." Normally, you can explain something to a player very quickly. Or, during the timeout you can go to coach and say, "Here's what your boy's doing out there." Let the coach instruct him. And you don't have to explain everything, but when kids repeatedly do something, there's a possibility they don't understand what they're doing.

NASO: How does judgment and discernment play into leadership?

Maxwell: They give you the ability to go one level beyond the rulebook. You know what the rules say, but you also have the ability to interpret a rule in the context of what is happening at the moment. If you called every infraction, there would be a thousand whistles in the game and it really wouldn't be played. Judgment and discernment allows the game to be played. Leadership is more than just technique; it's an art. The great leaders not only have the technique of leadership down and know the basics; they know the art of leadership. Just like when players are playing in the zone and everybody knows they're playing above their heads, a referee can be in the zone during a game as well.

NASO: What is the key characteristic of individuals who make good referees?

Maxwell: They have to see the whole picture, what's really transpiring. Your ability as a referee to not just see one individual issue, player or play, but constantly keep it in the context of what's the big picture is very important. For example, it's very easy to teach a referee how to recognize a foul on the basketball court, offside on a football team. It's very technical. It's more difficult to teach them how to make those calls in the context of the big picture, because that takes experience. In another of my books, *21 Irrefutable Laws of Leadership*, one of the laws is the law of intuition. It's the hardest law to teach, because you're intuitive in the area of your giftedness.

NASO: What does that mean?

Maxwell: Let's say that you have gifts of mercy and I'm hurting. Because you are gifted in that area, you'll quickly pick up that I'm hurting. Where if someone else didn't have that gift, they might go right by me. That's because it's in the area of giftedness. There are certain people who are going to be more naturally intuitive referees than others. That's a fact. There are some people who are born to referee — born to lead. But you're *intuitive* in the area of your giftedness, and you *grow* in the area of your experience. So what you do as an intuitive person without experience will not be very successful. If you find those people who are intuitively good at discernment or judgment and have the natural kind of leanings to being a good referee, they still must have game experience. As a result, it's very positive to put an inexperienced guy with the experienced guys. That's how they learn. What does an inexperienced person do? They watch the one who has the experience.

NASO: Why should referees work on team building?

Maxwell: One is too small of a number to achieve greatness. One referee out there on the field cannot do justice to the game. Teamwork is nothing more than identifying your niche — what is your strength. Because you know what? You have other referees with different strengths. The law of the big picture says the goal is more important than the rule. When you look at the qualities of a team player, you might say I'm not strong on all 17, but I'm strong on eight of them. When this cross-evaluation with other referees happens, there begins to be an understanding. You start to call the game not only based on who you are, but you call the game based on who the other referees are on the field.

NASO: Can leadership be shown in the way referees carry themselves?

Maxwell: If you go to an elevator and somebody gets on but never says a word, you can still tell if he or she has a good attitude.

When referees are on the field, they don't have to say a word. There are some whom you just want to go up and argue with — knock the chip off their shoulder. Then there are others who have more of a conciliatory, listening, let's reason together demeanor. I think that there's an air, a way that you carry yourself that shows whether you have gotten out of place as far as your position in a game. Referees should want to have body movements of confidence but not arrogance, and I think there's a difference between those.

John Maxwell is a well-known author who has written numerous books on leadership. Called "America's expert on leadership," Maxwell's books, tapes and seminars have influenced the lives of many. In addition, he is the founder of INJOY, an organization dedicated to helping people grow and reach their leadership capabilities. His publications are widely available at most booksellers.

5

Hot Topics Facing Officiating Leaders

In this chapter ...

• **Instant Replay**
  The pros and cons and where it's heading next.

• **Your Legal Rights and Responsibilities**
  Answers to your legal officiating questions.

In addition to discussing leadership issues throughout the majority of the 2005 NASO Summit, time was set aside devoted to some of the hottest topics in the officiating community. The issues of instant replay and the legal rights and responsibilities of sports officials were covered in depth.

Instant Replay

As countless coaches and players strive for excellence in sandlots, gyms and stadiums across the country, the quest for officiating perfection has increased the reach of instant replay.

To get a final say on whether a catch was made or a touchdown scored, technology is lending a hand more than ever. What was once solely a part of professional football — first in the USFL, then in the NFL — has found its way to the college game. The Big 10 Conference began a pilot program in 2003 by having a team of technical advisers attend games and file evaluations to determine the need for replay. Once the Big 10 received approval from the NCAA, the plan of working replay into regular-season games moved into full swing.

Now, it's at the high school level.

The Minnesota State High School League (MSHSL) board of directors ushered in the use of instant replay to the ranks of prep athletics at its Dec. 8, 2005, meeting, approving the use of instant replay in making critical calls during the high school hockey and basketball tournaments in March.

During the NASO Leadership Officiating Summit, panelists, including Dave Parry, the Big 10 supervisor of football officials and NCAA national coordinator of football officials; Ralph Swearngin, executive director of the Georgia High School Association; Tom Lepperd, the director of umpire administration for Major League Baseball; and Esse Baharmast, U.S. Soccer director of referee development, discussed the use of instant replay and its effectiveness in officiating.

Parry noted that taking the idea of replay from the drawing board to stadiums on Saturdays was not a short-term process. "We had brainstorming sessions, we had walk-throughs in spring games, walk-throughs in fall practices, met with the NFL, had them help us and did a great deal of homework," Parry says.

The move toward replay partially came as a reaction to a 2002 season that included a handful of high profile incidents when coaches and game officials did not see eye to eye.

Instant replay has come at a cost: Parry noted the price tag came to about $5,000 per school in the Big 10 to keep the program up and running in 2004. That amount covered both machinery expenses and additional pay to the technical advisers who had to take on added responsibilities.

"Our game length, which was a concern, how much longer is it going to stretch things out, went only three more minutes," Parry says. "We went from 3:13 to 3:16 and that included five overtimes. So really, the length of the game wasn't all that bad."

According to Parry, the cost and a minor stretch of time constraints turned out to be worth it for some increased piece of mind for all parties involved.

"The positive spin on it was that it created an element of trust," Parry pointed out. "Suddenly, our crowds became more tranquil. Our officials felt much safer getting off the field after a tough ballgame. Our coaches became more civil. We did not have near the rancor, the bitterness that we had before."

Since then, nearly all of the Division I college football conferences have followed suit, adopting similar replay plans with some variations. Instant replay was even in effect for the Bowl Championship Series this past season. In the Big 10, an official upstairs uses a paging system to notify five people on the field: the timer, referee, umpire, line judge and field judge. The referee then communicates with the replay official upstairs by phone.

Within the Big 10, the system gained an unprecedented show of support. Following the 2004 season, coaches voted 11-0 to keep replay. Athletic directors also voted unanimously to keep it.

The use of instant replay on the college level has prompted some discussion whether it would be feasible for high schools to set up something similar. Although some forms of replay usage had been proposed, especially for postseason games, no formal replay programs had been approved or made part of the high school scene at the time of the Summit.

That changed with Minnesota's late December announcement.

If all goes well with the Minnesota experiment, it's not a stretch to think that other state tournaments could follow suit. But right now, the use of instant replay in prep athletics is still controversial for several reasons.

One stumbling block for bringing replay to high school contests is that not all schools within a district or a state would have the necessary equipment or financial resources to create a uniform system. Swearngin feels the result would be an unbalanced playing field.

"We strongly believe that regular season all the way through the postseason, as much as possible, that all games be played by the same sort of rules and procedures. If we believe that technology with the replay review makes the game better, makes the sport better, then it seems unfair to only give the benefit of that improvement to places that are playing in adequate venues."

It would also be a necessity to have the proper equipment and camera positioning to provide a better look at the action than officials will have at field level. A handful of facilities in Georgia where some sectional tournaments and playoff games are held, such as the Georgia Dome, would be ready for replay.

In addition to the procedural challenges included in implementing a high school replay system, there is also the question of whether high school officials should operate under the same level of attention as a college or pro colleague.

"At the high school level, we are willing to live or die, sink or swim with the judgment call of officials, and I don't see it as an

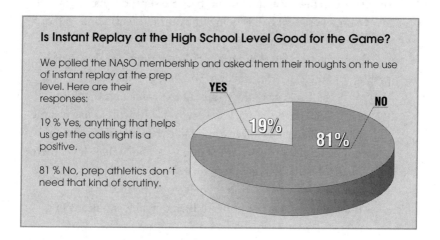

Is Instant Replay at the High School Level Good for the Game?

We polled the NASO membership and asked them their thoughts on the use of instant replay at the prep level. Here are their responses:

YES

NO

19 % Yes, anything that helps us get the calls right is a positive.

81 % No, prep athletics don't need that kind of scrutiny.

19%

81%

accountability issue," Swearngin said. "Accountability is to acquaint officials with a mistake that's made so that they would be less likely to make it in the future, not necessarily that we're going to stop the action and hold officials to a level of accountability, or a level of scrutiny, that we don't hold the other participants to who are equally human."

While replay has found a home in football, it is not used in a couple of other sports for a variety of reasons.

Major League Baseball's stance on instant replay can be summed up in a single sentence regulation found in the rulebook: "No electronic equipment, including television or videotape replay, shall be used to revise an umpire's decision or to assist an umpire in making a decision."

It is a position largely based on a tradition of baseball having had the element of human error as part of the equation. Instead of consulting a replay monitor, baseball umpires have adopted an onfield policy of getting together to discuss a call when an individual asks the other members of his crew for assistance. Umpires are also instructed to follow a short rule that every batter has heard hundreds of times: Keep your eye on the ball.

"We encourage the umpires to get together on controversial plays. All four of you guys, get away from the managers, the players, talk it over and take a quick breather," said Lepperd. "We also tell all umpires to keep your eye on the ball, which sometimes means if you happen to have the responsibility for watching a runner touch the base, that would become secondary and you keep an eye on where that ball is going, the outfield fence, or a trap or a catch, something like that."

Many of the sports pondering replay options are able to fit a system into the flow of the action. Soccer is an exception.

"In soccer, because of the nature of the game and the fluidity that is involved in the game, it is very, very difficult to use instant replay," said Baharmast. "We don't have the natural breaks. In soccer, when the ball goes out of bounds, at the highest level there are 10 balls. There are ball boys who get another ball back and the ball is immediately in play, so there is no stoppage."

Although replay is not utilized during match situations in

soccer, it can be used as a disciplinary tool after a match. If a referee does not see a foul that causes a player injury, officials can review tape and hand out subsequent fines or suspensions.

During the 1994 World Cup, a defender who elbowed another player, breaking his nose, was suspended for nine games and fined. FIFA officials are now experimenting with a microchip in a soccer ball that will emit a beeping sound to signal that a ball has crossed a line.

As for the future prospects of instant replay in general, Baharmast feels its viability will be tied to economic factors.

"I think at the highest level where there's a lot of money on the line, I think that is what's driving this," said Baharmast. "Eventually, I think the people who are trying to get perfection, because perfection means millions of dollars either going this way or the other way, will try to force it."

Baharmast noted that giving replay too much importance could compromise some important life lessons for younger athletes.

"Part of going to high school and college is to learn that life is not always fair," Baharmast said. "Sometimes things are thrown your way that you have to accept and say, 'You know, it wasn't fair. I've got to get up and I've got to move on.' It becomes a philosophical question."

Attempts to start up instant replay systems below the Division I level of college football may also be hampered by money issues.

"We've heard some discussion on Division II and Division III, but it becomes such an economic issue," Parry said. "Plus, those schools often don't have the physical facilities to do that. Probably where there are big bucks, you're going to see replay. That's probably inevitable."

Lepperd agreed that financial considerations will likely prevent instant replay from being practical at the collegiate or minor league level for baseball. But money could make replay's presence known in the majors.

"At the Major League level, I think eventually you'll see some form of it. Because the money's there, I think eventually you'll see something with it."

Your Legal Rights and Responsibilities

A player gets hurt, a fight breaks out, someone wants to do a background check on you and all sorts of other situations arise in which you need advice from a lawyer. NASO provides its members with free access to attorneys through its Legal Information and Consultation Program (LICP), and even conducted a face-to-face legal question-and-answer session at last summer's Leadership Officiating Summit in Salt Lake City. Alan Goldberger, the nation's leading expert on legal issues in officiating, and Lowell Gratigny, senior vice president in charge of legal services for American Specialty, NASO's insurance provider, were on hand to answer attendees' legal questions.

Lack of Security

Question: Can I sue a school that constantly fails to provide me a locker room, some sort of security, and even a game manager to work with me when I get to the game?

Goldberger: Most of us, me included, have really wanted to sue a school for failure to provide all those things that you mention. Unfortunately, or fortunately as the case may be, the legal system doesn't provide a remedy for every injustice. Obviously, failing to have proper facilities at a school is something that is a chronic complaint of all of us. I would say the best way to address that particular situation is through your local association. Have your group petition the schools and conferences to remedy the situation.

Background Checks

Question: We just had legislation passed by the state of Florida that all officials submit to a background check and be fingerprinted. If the official refuses to pay the money for a background check and the school board refuses them work, can the official sue them?

Goldberger: The practical problem is if it's a state statute, which is the case in Florida, there aren't going to be a whole lot of ways to get around that. So if the law says if you want a license as an official, if you have to pay X amount of dollars and undergo the test, whether it's fingerprinting or appearing at the police station, then you pretty much have to do it or you're not going to referee.

The only way that would change is if a legislature repealed it or if somebody were to bring a lawsuit and say that's unconstitutional, that's unlawful for whatever reason they can conjure up and if they can convince a judge to overturn the statute.

Question: Even if state law or the state association doesn't require a background check on officials, could our local association conduct background checks on our members anyway?

Goldberger: Every referee association in the country wants to do the right thing, right? Every association in the country feels that background checks are something that's coming because of all the problems we keep hearing about on the news and some of the high profile incidents that have come about as a result of those who were supervising youth sports and interscholastic sports. The problem is that for your officials association, you cannot run off doing background checks unless and until, one, you know what you're looking for; number two, you have a legally sound method of performing the check; and number three, you have a good idea of what you're going to do with the information when you get it. The best advice we can give to officials associations at this point in time with regard to background checks is this: Look around to the schools and the leagues you are servicing. Look around to the programs that you're involved with. If somebody else is doing background checks, let them. If you insist on doing background checks, you had better get some legal advice before you get started, and you'd better be careful what you ask for because you may just get it. Do your bylaws provide what the requirements are? Suppose somebody doesn't consent to a background check. Do they have to? Is it legal in your state to even do it and under what circumstances? And then what are the kinds of things for which officials can be disqualified from working? Is it drunk driving? Is it child abuse? Is it armed robbery? Is it passing a bad check? The point is you have to know exactly what you're doing before you get started, or don't get started.

Unsafe Conditions

Question: If we have an unsafe condition in a basketball gym or arena and management says they cannot make it safe, do we have the right to refuse to work that game? Suppose there are 1,500-2,000 fans in the stands and the school has collected a lot from the gate, can a school or a district come after us for that if we don't work?

Goldberger: I don't care how many tickets have been sold. I don't care if there's a sword swallower lined up at halftime. If it's unsafe and it can't be corrected and it presents an unreasonable risk to the student-athlete, there is no game. You're the referee. I guarantee if you play the game under those circumstances and a student-athlete or anybody else is injured, everybody in the western hemisphere will testify that we played this game because the referee said it was OK. So you can either tell it to the jury or you can consider the safety of the players.

Players Fighting

Question: When it comes to fights during games, I've heard the philosophy that you don't ever touch players and I've heard that you've got to get between players. What guidelines can you offer and how does it impact my liability insurance coverage?

Gratigny: I see fights erupting between players and parents and officials more now than I have even two, three or four years ago. It seems like they're breaking out at a younger age group. You can't buy insurance for intentional acts. Our NASO policy expands that a little bit. We provide coverage to an official who is trying to protect persons or property. So if a father comes up and threatens to hit you over the head with a baseball bat and you protect yourself, you would have full coverage under the policy to do that. I'll let Alan address whether it's best to touch players or not.

Goldberger: "Never touch a player." Almost everybody has heard that. We can't put our hands on a player because we'll get sued. In my view there is little that is further from the truth or from good officiating mechanics than the advice to never touch a player. If you let players fight because you're standing around and taking numbers, your game is down the toilet. If you let them see your stripes and let them see that you're there and between them, if you save the fight, you save your ballgame, and you may save yourself a lawsuit. Go over it in your pregame. One thing is for sure: You move quickly, you get in between the opponents and you don't let the fight happen. And if it does happen, you do whatever you can to stop it as quickly as you can. Does that mean you have to put your hands on somebody? I think it does. It's the only answer, folks.

Question: What about a postgame situation, in which the officials have not left the confines of the playing area? Should we handle a fight differently in a postgame situation?

Goldberger: The first thing we have to look at is the official's jurisdiction. We are on duty until we no longer have jurisdiction for the game. There's a timeline there that we have to deal with. You want to do what's reasonable under the circumstances. Get the final score straight and then get out fast. If a fight breaks out before then, you still have jurisdiction and have to deal with it. The best advice is to get out as soon as you are legally entitled to get out, when your jurisdiction is over. If it isn't, keep looking because you're still the referee.

Gratigny: I'll add an example. One of the worst fights I've heard of happened down in Florida. It happened during the good sportsmanship handshake after a football game. Someone brought suit against the officials and we ended up convincing the court that once a game was over the officials didn't have any right or duty to control the teams that ended up pummeling each other. So from a legal standpoint, the officials were not liable.

Doctor's Notes

Question: I'm looking for some direction when it comes to doctors' notes indicating that a player can play. We have privacy issues in our state dealing with keeping the note. Could you give a legal interpretation whether the official should keep the note or whether just seeing the note is good enough?

Goldberger: There was case like that just a few seasons ago in which a high school football referee was presented with a note from the team physician indicating that a particular student could play with the apparatus or the cast or the bandage or whatever it was in accordance with the NFHS rulebook. That was good and fine, so the note was displayed to the referee, and the referee says, "Fine, thank you," and he reaches for it. But the nurse says, "No, you can't have it." The referee says, "Why not?" And the nurse says it's because of medical privacy laws. Well, the referee correctly concluded that if it was OK for him to see it, it was OK for him — and in fact necessary for him — to take a copy of it. I think that's where the answer is. If there is a situation in which the student-athlete needs a note from a physician or anybody else to play, or there's some writing that has to be produced, most legal authorities would say you'd better hold onto it.

Gratigny: And the reason for keeping the note is because a minor can bring suit once they reach the age of majority plus whatever that statute of limitations is. So officials can get nailed with lawsuits six, seven, eight years down the road. We don't get many of them, because generally the suits that last that long are bad injury suits, and we're generally aware of the kids that get injured pretty seriously. But a lawsuit is a lawsuit, so those records have to be maintained for a long period of time.

Appendix I

NASO Sports Officiating Summit 2005
Session List

ARE YOU LEADERSHIP MATERIAL? — Longtime NBA referee Bob Delaney knows a thing or two about leadership — on the court and off it. Not only an NBA crew chief, Delaney spent the first half of his working life as a New Jersey State trooper, working undercover to bring down key mob figures and then serving as a hostage negotiator. Here, he set the stage for our two-day discussion on leadership officiating, showing how to bring out the leader in any official and illuminating the differences between a leader and a manager. Attendees discovered the many ways leadership skills carry through your life and how they especially serve you in officiating.

WHAT LEAD OFFICIALS DO BETTER THAN THE REST — Attendees experienced the unique opportunity to hear the secrets of the very best officials working at the highest levels of competition. Among the lead officials featured are NFL referee Bill Carollo, who officiated Super Bowls XXX and XXXVII; NBA referees Violet Palmer and Joe Crawford, a man who has worked the NBA finals 19 straight years; and NCAA national coordinator of baseball umpires Dave Yeast. *Referee* magazine Vice President Bill Topp moderated this no-holds barred discussion on what makes lead officials tick.

IT'S A WHOLE NEW BALLGAME: THE EXPANDING RESPONSIBILITIES OF SPORTS OFFICIALS — Let's face it, compared to years past there is a lot more expected of officials. Not only is there an increased emphasis on training and education, but these days it seems we officials are expected to be part medical doctor, part meteorologist, part fashion police and most anything else that's convenient to foist on us that has nothing to do with actual officiating. How and why we're being saddled with all sorts of additional responsibilities — and the potential legal liability that accompanies each — are the key questions addressed by our panel consisting of NASO President Barry Mano, NFHS Assistant Executive Director Mary Struckhoff, Southland Conference Baseball Umpire Supervisor and Big 12 football referee Jon Bible, Coordinator of Men's Basketball Officials for five NCAA Division I conferences Dale Kelley and moderator Ken Allan, an NCAA Division I baseball umpire and radio personality.

BETTER TALK TO A LAWYER: YOUR QUESTIONS ANSWERED — We touched on the potential liabilities associated with officiating in the "It's a Whole New Ballgame" session. Attendees had the opportunity to get any and all of their legal officiating questions answered by some of NASO's Legal Information and Consultation Program (LICP) experts. Alan Goldberger, amateur sports official and New Jersey attorney specializing in sports officiating and the law, and Lowell Gratigny, American Specialty Insurance Services, Inc., senior vice president of litigation management, joined moderator Steven Ellinger, executive director of the Texas Association of Sports Officials.

REPLAY — COMING TO YOUR GAME SOON! — When the NFL pioneered the use of instant video replay technology back in 1986, it was a revolution in the way people viewed sports and officials called games. Since then, video technology has popped up in the NBA, NCAA basketball and football and the NHL, and it's been a talking point in nearly every other sport and competition level — including high school games. Panelists Ralph Swearngin, Georgia High School Association executive director; Tom Lepperd, Major League Baseball director of umpire administration; Esse Baharmast, USSF director of advanced and international referee development; and Dave Parry, Big 10 supervisor of football officials, as well as moderator Jim Arehart, *Referee* magazine senior managing editor, discussed the pros and cons of the all-seeing video replays — and when you'll see them in your games.

OFFICIATING ON TAP — Unwind after day one of the NASO Summit over cocktails and conversation with any one of nine hot officiating topics, such as sportsmanship, recruiting and retention, selecting postseason officials and local association management. Select a seat from a variety of tables, each manned by a topic facilitator. That free-flowing happy-hour setting event allowed attendees to set up camp at any one of the tables or move around gleaning a little something from each topic of conversation.

THE ART OF VERBAL JUDO —You may have heard of Verbal Judo before now and it would be no surprise since it has been around for 23 years and is used by more than 700 law enforcement agencies worldwide. For the first time Dr. George Thompson, founder and president of the Verbal Judo Institute, brought his proven seminar on conflict resolution to sports officiating. He taught skills for defusing a heated conversation with a coach or a player quickly, effectively and non-confrontationally. He also showed when it's time to stop talking and act.

HELP OFFICIALS BUY INTO YOUR VISION —You're an assigner, supervisor, commissioner, local association board member or a crew chief and you have any number of officials you are responsible for. How do you get a disparate group of individuals to all follow the leader? That's the question posed to panelists NFL Director of Officiating Mike Pereira, NCAA National Coordinator of Baseball Umpires Dave Yeast, NFHS Basketball Rules Chair and Kentucky High School Athletic Association Assistant Commissioner Larry Boucher and NCAA Coordinator of Women's Basketball Officials Marcy Weston, along with moderator Professional Association of Volleyball Officials President Joan Powell.

HOW WE MAKE THINGS WORSE — When it comes to officials, supervisors probably have a few things to get off their chests. When it comes to supervisors, officials probably have a few things to get off theirs. No matter what areas of officiating you're involved in — assigning, local association leadership, the state office, oncourt or onfield officiating — everyone has gripes. Here was your chance to talk about them. But don't think that was just an exercise in catharsis. Solutions were discussed. *Referee* Assistant Editor Keith Zirbel and Associate Editor Ken Koester identified the major problem areas and looked for potential solutions to those problems.

THE 8 CRITICAL CHALLENGES WE MUST OVERCOME NOW! — Whether you're a working official or officiating administrator, you didn't want to miss the finale. *Referee* magazine Senior Editor Jeffrey Stern moderated as panelists Ronnie Carter, Tennessee Secondary School Athletic Association executive director; Jerry McGee, Wingate University president and major college football official; Anita Ortega, major college women's basketball official, and Jerry Seeman, NFL officiating consultant, NASO chair and former NFL senior director of officiating, discussed each of the eight critical challenges and why we must all address them today.

Appendix II

NASO Sports Officiating Summit 2005 Speaker List

Ken Allan — Sports broadcaster for the American Forces Radio Network; California state baseball rules interpreter; California Interscholastic Federation-Southern Section instructional chairman; former assistant commissioner for the Southern California Collegiate Baseball Umpires Association; worked four NCAA Division II College World Series; retired 30-year NCAA Division I umpire; Referee contributor.

Marcia Alterman — Professional Association of Volleyball Officials executive director, rules interpreter and former president; named first NCAA women's volleyball rules interpreter in 2002; numerous postseason assignments at all levels of collegiate volleyball; Big 10 Conference and Conference USA coordinator of volleyball officials; Officiating Development Alliance member.

Jim Arehart — Referee Enterprises, Inc., senior managing editor; high school football official.

Esse Baharmast — USSF director of advanced and international referee development; former USSF director of officials; retired international referee; worked two 1998 World Cup matches in France; became the first American referee to whistle two World Cup matches; recipient of 1997 MLS Referee of the Year Award; worked 1996 Olympic games; NASO board member.

Larry Boucher — Kentucky High School Athletic Association assistant commissioner; NFHS Basketball Rules Committee chair; former commissioner and supervisor of basketball officials for the Kentucky Intercollegiate Athletic Conference; former Division I and high school basketball official; former high school basketball supervisor and assigner.

Jerry Bovee — Utah High School Activities Association assistant director, coordinates Utah officials and coaches training programs; NFHS Football Rules Committee member.

Bill Carollo — National Football League Referees Association president; NFL official; worked Super Bowls XXX and XXXVII; former NCAA Division I basketball official; NASO board member-elect.

Ronnie Carter — Tennessee Secondary School Athletic Association executive director; former high school teacher, coach, official and administrator; served on many committees, including the NFHS Football, Basketball and Wrestling Rules Committees; past president of the NFHS board of directors; NASO board member.

Joe Crawford — NBA referee; NBA Finals referee every year since 1986; has worked more NBA playoff and Finals games than any current NBA official; worked three All Star games; son of former MLB umpire Shag Crawford and brother to current MLB umpire Jerry Crawford.

Bob Delaney — NBA referee; 2003 NASO Gold Whistle Award winner; worked NBA Finals six times; former National Basketball Referees Association executive board member.

Steven Ellinger — Texas Association of Sports Officials executive director; NBA officials observer; Referee contributor; former chair of the Entertainment and Sports Law Section of the State Bar of Texas; high school, college and international basketball official.

Alan Goldberger — Sports law attorney and recognized legal authority for game officials; author of *Sports Officiating: A Legal Guide*; Legal Information and Consultation Program representative; frequent speaker to groups of game officials, coaches, recreation professionals and attorneys; member, counsel and chair of many officials associations; Referee contributor; former baseball and football official; former NCAA Division I basketball official.

Lowell Gratigny — American Specialty Insurance Services, Inc., senior vice president, claims management, NASO's insurance agency; Legal Information and Consultation Program representative.

Marty Hickman — Illinois High School Association executive director; NFHS Strategic Planning Team chair.

Ben Jay — Pac-10 assistant commissioner; former high school basketball official.

James Jorgensen — Owner of Jorgensen Sports Service, an assigning company; California Officials Association director; former Columbia Football Association and Northern California Athletic Conference commissioner; former Division I basketball official; former NASO board member.

Bob Kanaby — NFHS executive director; former New Jersey State Interscholastic Athletic Association (NJSIAA) executive director; leader in production of the Citizenship Through Sports and Fine Arts Curriculum; USA Basketball's Constitution and Bylaws Committee chair; Naismith Basketball Hall of Fame board member; former football rules committee member; NJSIAA Award of Honor recipient and Hall of Fame inductee; Ohio High School Athletic Association Ethics and Integrity award winner.

Dale Kelley — Conference USA, Big 12, Sun Belt and Southland Conference men's basketball coordinator of officials; worked nine consecutive NCAA basketball tournaments, including Final Fours in 1978 and 1981; inducted into the Bethel College Hall of Fame, Tennessee Secondary Schools Athletic Association Hall of Fame, Carroll County Sports Hall of Fame, Tennessee Sports Hall of Fame and received Bethel College's Outstanding Alumni Achievement Award; mayor of his hometown, Huntingdon, Tenn.

Ken Koester — Referee Enterprises, Inc., associate editor with specific responsibility for basketball coverage; high school and small college basketball official; high school and small college football official; former high school baseball umpire.

Tom Lepperd — Major League Baseball director of umpire administration; former minor league umpire; AL regular season fill-in from 1984-86; Umpire Development

Program member; former NL assistant director of umpires; Officiating Development Alliance member.

Barry Mano — NASO founder and president; Referee Enterprises, Inc., founder and president; Referee magazine publisher; former NCAA Division I basketball official; Officiating Development Alliance member.

Jerry McGee — Wingate University president; NCAA Division I football official; worked 14 bowl games, including two national championship games; NCAA Division II Football Issue Committee national chairman; former NCAA President's Council member.

Tim Millis — Big 12 Conference coordinator of football officials; former NFL official, worked Super Bowls XXIX and XXXIII.

Anita Ortega — Los Angeles Police Department commanding officer; NCAA Division I women's basketball official; inducted into the UCLA Athletic Hall of Fame; worked the Pac-10 women's basketball tournament in 2002; worked eight consecutive NCAA women's basketball tournaments; 1978 UCLA women's basketball national championship team member; NASO board member.

Violet Palmer — NBA referee; former NCAA Division I women's basketball referee; worked women's Final Four four times, including two national championship games; NASO board member-elect.

Dave Parry — CAA national coordinator of football officials; Big 10 coordinator of football officials; National Football Foundation and College Hall of Fame Outstanding Football Official Award winner; retired 15-year NFL official; former major college official; worked Super Bowl XVII.

Mike Pereira — NFL director of officiating; former NFL supervisor and Western Athletic Conference supervisor of officials; retired NFL and NCAA Division I football official; worked eight college bowl games; Officiating Development Alliance member.

Joan Powell — Professional Association of Volleyball Officials president; longtime high school teacher, coach and volleyball official; five-time NCAA Division I volleyball Final Four referee; former national Association of Girls and Women in Sport rules committee member; former NFHS rules committee member; NASO board secretary.

Marc Ratner — Nevada State Athletic Commission executive director; commissioner of high school officials in southern Nevada; NCAA Division I football official; high school basketball official; former high school softball umpire; NASO board vice chair.

Ed T. Rush — Former NBA director of officiating and director of officiating programs; involved with NBA officiating recruitment and development; co-founder of Coast to Coast Referee School; retired NBA referee; worked 34 Finals, five All-Star games, more than 240 playoff and 2,100 regular season games; former NASO board chair; former ODA member.

Jerry Seeman — NFL consultant; retired NFL senior director of officiating; retired

NFL official; numerous postseason assignments, including Super Bowls XXIII and XXV; officiated high school and college football and basketball for 22 years; 2001 NASO Mel Narol Medallion Award winner; NASO board chair.

Jeffrey Stern — Referee Enterprises, Inc., senior editor with specific responsibility for football and baseball coverage; high school and college football official; high school baseball umpire; former basketball, wrestling and softball official.

Mary Struckhoff — NFHS assistant director; NFHS basketball and softball rules interpreter and editor; NFHS Officials Association and Officials Education Program staff liaison; NCAA Division I women's basketball and former high school volleyball official; former Illinois High School Association assistant executive director; Officiating Development Alliance member.

Ralph Swearngin — Georgia High School Association executive director; NFHS Softball Rules Committee chair; NFHS Football Rules Committee member; National Christian College Athletic Association Hall of Fame member; former high school football official; former basketball and baseball college coach.

George Thompson — Verbal Judo Institute president and founder; author of three books on conflict management and resolution.

Bill Topp — Referee Enterprises, Inc., vice president publishing and managing services; high school and college basketball and high school football official; former NCAA Division I baseball umpire and small college football official; 2000 NCAA Division III World Series umpire; Officiating Development Alliance member.

Mark Uyl — Michigan High School Athletic Association assistant director responsible for programming and services for Michigan officials; high school baseball umpire and football official.

Marcy Weston — Central Michigan University senior associate athletic director; NCAA national coordinator of women's basketball officiating; worked 1982 and 1984 NCAA women's basketball championships; Women's Basketball Hall of Fame inductee; named in 1991 as one of nine major contributors to first decade of NCAA women's basketball; former NASO board member and chair; Officiating Development Alliance member.

Dave Yeast — NCAA national coordinator of baseball umpires; Amateur Baseball Umpires Association board member; former NCAA Division I umpire; former Missouri Valley and Conference USA supervisor of baseball umpires; worked two College World Series and the 1996 Olympics; Officiating Development Alliance member.

Henry Zaborniak Jr. — Ohio High School Athletic Association assistant commissioner; NCAA Division I football official; former collegiate women's and men's basketball and former NFL Europe official; NASO board member.

Keith Zirbel — Referee Enterprises, Inc., editorial operations manager; high school and college football official; high school basketball official and baseball umpire.